HOW TO
CHECK
AND
CORRECT
COLOR
PROOFS

0%   Balance Kreuzmiren   c   50%

0,5%	1%
2%	3%
4%	5%

6µ
8µ
11
13
16

% 50% Balance Kreuzmiren C

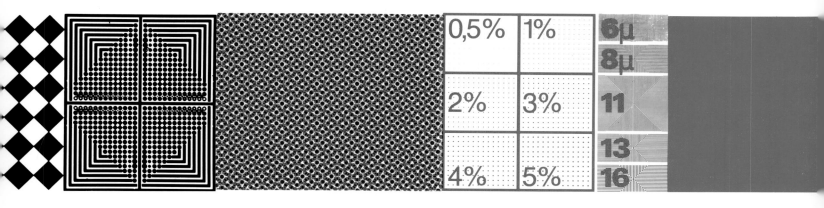

0,5%	1%
2%	3%
4%	5%

6μ
8μ
11
13
16

HOW TO
CHECK
AND
CORRECT
COLOR
PROOFS

DAVID BANN
&
JOHN GARGAN

50% 50%

NORTH
LIGHT
BOOKS

M 50

A QUARTO BOOK

First published in the U.S.A. by
North Light Books, an imprint of
F & W Publications, Inc
1507 Dana Avenue
Cincinnati, Ohio 45207

First published 1990
Copyright© 1990
Quarto Publishing plc

ISBN 0–89134–350–4

This book was designed and produced
by Quarto Publishing plc,
The Old Brewery, 6 Blundell Street,
London N7 9BH

Consultants Duncan Ross,
Tony Farquharson

Senior Editor Kate Kirby
Editors Eleanor Van Zandt, Richard
Dawes

Design Nick Çlark
Picture Research Arlene Bridgewater
Illustrator David Kemp
Photographers Martin Norris,
Ian Howes, Paul Forrester

Art Director Moira Clinch
Assistant Art Director
Chloë Alexander

Special thanks go to
Grey Matter Design Consultants

The images in this book have been
proofed to the highest possible
standards. However, it should be
remembered that color correction is
a subjective area open to individual
interpretation.
The color bars reproduced in this
book are for use as a guide only. They
cannot be used for checking against
color proofs.
This book contains examples of
graphic design work. These examples
are included for the purpose of
criticism and review.

Typeset by Ampersand
Typesetting Limited, Bournemouth
Manufactured in Hong Kong by
Regent Publishing Services Limited
Printed in Singapore by
Tien Wah Press (Pte) Limited.

Balance Kreuzmiren C 50%

CONTENTS

All about proofs

This section explains what the four-color process can achieve. The different methods of proofing are shown, as well as how the color separation house produces final film and carries out corrections.

How to check color proofs

This section explains in detail what the designer should look for when checking proofs; the equipment required; how to mark up proofs; and what color bars are used for.

Examples are shown of proofs that are up or down in each of the four process colors or incorrect in other ways. Different subjects can present very different reproduction problems, and a range is given, showing what can go wrong and how to correct it.

0%   25%

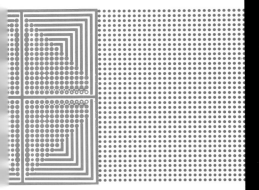

This linen tester is used throughout the book to show enlargements of particular details. The enlargement is usually 300%.

Use your own linen tester to look at other areas of the subjects and to familiarize yourself with which characteristics are important in achieving the final printed result.

M

DAVID BANN is a graduate of the London College of Printing and a member of the Institute of Printing. He works on the production side of book publishing and is a director of Landmark Production Consultants. He has lectured extensively on book production and is the author of the *Print Production Handbook*.

WHEN REPRODUCING a piece of work for printing, the client, the designer, and the color separation house may not have the same priorities. The client will want the job to look as good as possible, come in at the budgeted price, and be delivered on time. The designer will also want the job to look as good as possible, but this priority may overshadow those of cost and schedule. The color separation house has to translate the designer's concept into something that can be printed, and wants to make a profit and retain the client.

When things go wrong, it is nearly always due to poor communication between the three parties. This book is an attempt to improve communication by helping the designer to present artwork and layouts in the best way for the color house and to mark up proofs so as to get the best possible results.

The designer's work does not stop at the layout stage; input is needed up to and during separation, proofing, and printing. A good design will not succeed unless it can be translated effectively into the final printed job. I hope this book will help designers and color houses to work as partners rather than, as sometimes happens, as adversaries.

David Bann
May 1990

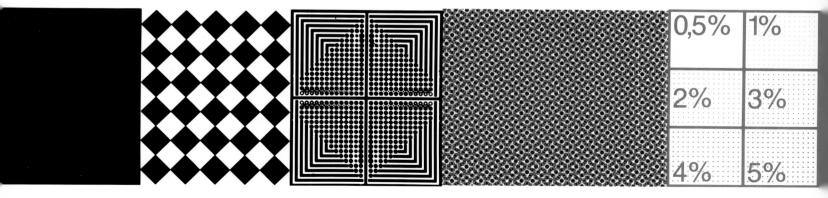

I HAVE BEEN in color separation longer than I care to remember, and in that time the industry has improved immensely. Better technology means that work can be reproduced more quickly, more efficiently, and to a higher standard.

Today's designers are rightly more demanding, and the industry has kept pace with their expectations. Also, there is now a better understanding between designers and color separation houses. If it is the designer's vision that makes a printed job, it is the color house's skills that help to realize that vision in the finished work.

Most of the content of this book is not taught in graphic design courses, and until now the designer has had to learn through first-hand experience. Here, David and I have tried to offer a short-cut to this knowledge. We have tried not to blind you with science but simply to give you the basic facts about proof correction and how to get the best from your color house.

When a color house has done a good job, it is always a pleasure to be told so, but we can also accept criticism when it is justified. As an industry, we do listen.

JOHN GARGAN has thirty years' experience in color separation. He started his career as a color planner and now runs Colour Solutions, a separation house associated with Omnicom, one of the largest communication companies in the world.

John Gargan
May 1990

en   C   50%   50%   25%   75%

Sending material to the color house

THREE CRITERIA govern the selection of a supplier – price, quality, and service. Each of these aspects is discussed below.

PRICE In color separation, prices can vary a lot from one supplier to another, depending on location, equipment, and type of work undertaken.

Color separation suppliers can be found in large cities and country areas across the U.S., as well as in Europe and the Far East. The schedule will determine whether the work can be placed abroad or even outside the town or city where the client and designer are located. Courier services enable packages to be in other parts of the U.S. the next day and in the Far East in a maximum of 48 hours. However, the timing of many jobs is so critical that work must be dealt with the same day, which restricts the choice to local color houses.

In practice, color separation is done abroad only on large jobs such as books or catalogues where there is an extended schedule. A typical separation house in Singapore or Hong Kong will reproduce and proof 200 transparencies in 14 days including transit time, and at a cost considerably lower than U.S. prices. However, this is the first proof stage, and after this time must be allowed for checking and returning the proofs and seeing reproofs of some subjects before the production of final film. Checking and correction can extend the total time for a large job to three to four weeks. Another factor is that color separation houses outside large cities are usually cheaper because of lower rates of pay. Price is also related to service, and although separation houses that work around the clock have to pay (and charge) more for shift work, they can often turn jobs around overnight.

QUALITY The quality offered by a color separation house depends on the equipment it has, as well as on the ability of the staff and their experience in dealing with the type of work in hand. Some color houses specialize in book work, some in packaging, and some in magazines or corporate work, such as company annual reports.

To establish a color separation house's quality, you can ask to see samples, visit the factory, or get the recommendation of other customers. The last option is probably the best guide, for if someone whose opinion you respect has used a color house over a period of time and can recommend it, that firm should be considered. The printer you are using for the job will have experience of different color houses and should also be in a position to recommend several.

SERVICE A color separation house that provides good service will meet all the proof dates and the date for final film and, if possible, will make up time if jobs run late at any stage. Good service also means

1 How long until first proofs?
2 On approval, how long until final film?
3 Have you done work of this nature and can you show me samples?
4 Who are your main customers?
5 What equipment do you have?
6 Do you work 24 hours a day?
7 Have you won any awards for your work?
8 Do you collect and deliver?

responding quickly to inquiries and paying close attention to detail. Service is obviously of vital importance on dated items such as magazines.

SPECIFICATION When you have shortlisted three or four color separation houses that can meet the price, quality, and service criteria, the next step is to draw up a specification for the job (see opposite).

The specification for separation should indicate the number of originals, whether they are transparencies or flat artworks, the size at which they are to appear, whether or not any of the originals are "in pro" (in proportion – that is, to the same percentage reduction or enlargement; see pages 40–41), the page size, whether pictures bleed, whether proofs are to be scatter or page proofs, and the number and type of proofs required, e.g. Cromalins or wet proofs (see pages 56–57).

Black and white pictures should be described as halftone or line. The final product required should be stated (e.g. scanned sets or final positives and whether random or paged). Where wet proofs are being produced, the separation house should always be asked to supply progressives (see pages 58–59) to the printer. With wet proofing, the specification should include the type of paper required.

Always state how long the prices should be valid, as color separation houses have periodic increases because of pay increases or inflation. If you can send a copy of the layout, this will greatly help the color house to prepare an accurate estimate.

THE ESTIMATE When you receive the color separation house's estimate, check carefully that it accords with the specification. Most color houses request to see the mechanical on their estimate, in case any subjects need special treatment. If possible, include any such requirements in the specification.

If the prospective suppliers all offer the same standard of quality and service, the one quoting the

---

A brochure   From: A customer   To: A color separation house

Please quote for separation and proofing to the following specification:

Trimmed Page Size: 8½ × 11, full bleeds   ¡Extent: 32 pages self-cover

8 black and white halftones (× half-page) out of pro
10 black and white line illustrations (× quarter-page) in pro
20 transparencies out of pro – sizes as follows:
8 × full-page
6 × half-page
6 × quarter-page
Rules and tint-laying as attached layout
Type supplied as camera-ready copy in page form

Please supply 12 sets of page proofs in double-page spreads on 90 lb matte-coated paper. On approval, supply final film positives, right-reading emulsion-down, in page form and progressives. Make prices valid to December 1990.

SPEC SHEET FOR A COLOR HOUSE

---

lowest price will normally get the work. However, prices are usually negotiable, and if you are eager to give the work to a particular color house, you may be able to negotiate the price down to match that offered by a competitor.

When the designer requotes the selected supplier's price to the client, it is wise to add a contingency of 10% or more to allow for unforeseen problems.

EXTRAS Once the job is in hand, extra costs ("extras") may arise for a number of reasons. It is important, where any major extra work is required, that the separation house advise you before carrying it out, so that you can inform the client and avoid a three-way argument at invoice stage. A common area of contention is reproofing. In cases where the original proof was not up to standard, the separation house should not charge the cost of reproofing. However, it is justified in charging if the designer changes the size or asks for a different color result than in the original.

Originals for reproduction

Transcript for the image caption:

Transparencies should always be protected by a plastic sleeve.
Glass mounts should be removed as they may break in transit and damage the original. Flat artwork should be covered to protect the surface.
Never use paper-clips on halftone originals as the scanner picks up the impression and it can appear on the proof.

THE COLOR HOUSE needs good originals to do a good job, and the careful selection and preparation of these is a vital component of a successful result.

LINE ORIGINALS Unlike most photographs for reproduction, line originals are often specially commissioned, which means that when briefing the artist you can make sure that they are prepared in the most suitable way for reproduction.

A line original should be black, and may be drawn larger than the size at which it is to appear, in which case any slight inaccuracies in the artwork will be minimized when it is reduced. It should be mounted on stable board and should include trim and bleed marks. Tints can be laid by the artist, but tints laid by the color house are usually cleaner, though slightly more expensive.

Any alterations or corrections to drawings should be free of blemishes. Watch for this particularly where the artist has made a correction.

You can give the size either as a linear measurement (e.g. reduce width to 4 inches) or as a percentage reduction or enlargement (e.g. reduce to 66% of original size). Same-size reproduction may be indicated by "S/S." The required crop can be shown by a traced overlay to the correct dimensions.

TYPE Typeset material is treated like a line original by the reproduction process. CRC (camera-ready copy) should be mounted on a base firm enough to prevent any stuck-down copy becoming detached if the base is flexed. Stable but flexible board is a suitable base for most jobs. Where type is set as complete pages of bromide with nothing stuck down, it does not require a base.

Grids should be printed in pale, non-reproducing blue, and the same color should be used by the designer for any written instructions on the CRC. (The camera will pick up any other color and the color house will have to touch it out on the film.)

It is important that the setting itself be correctly exposed and developed, to give a sharp image of consistent density. Where correction lines have been stripped in, make sure that they are the same density as the initial setting. If there is a correction to just one line, it is better to reset a "patch" of three or four lines, as this will prevent or at least reduce any density variation.

Where type is reversed out of color or over-prints a color, particular care must be taken (see pages 132–133).

COLOR PHOTOGRAPHS These can either be transparencies or prints, the former giving a brighter, sharper result. The original should have reasonable contrast, and there should be no overall color cast. (However, if there is a color cast and no alternative original is available, the color house can be alerted to it and will probably be able to lose it in scanning – see page 37.) Images with excessive grain should be avoided, as this will show up, particularly if the picture is enlarged. A big enlargement can cause problems, especially when it is from a 35mm original (see pages 40–41).

Original transparencies should be used where possible, since duplicating a transparency increases density. The sizing of transparencies is done in the same way as for black and white line and half-tone work.

In the absence of any instructions, the color separation house will attempt to match the transparency, so if the designer requires something to be altered (such as losing a color cast or making a transparency brighter), it is important to mention it when the job is begun, rather than at proof stage.

Where color is important, as in photographs of works of art, the photographer will include a color scale in the transparency outside the area to be used. This scale is called a color-control patch and indicates any color bias there may be in the transparency. This bias may be caused by a mismatch between the lighting conditions and the film or may be due to the natural fading of a transparency, which tends to occur over a period of time. These patches are useful both in the processing of film and to alert the color separation house to any color cast.

BLACK AND WHITE HALFTONES Photographs to be reproduced as halftones should have good contrast and detail (see pages 82–83) and be free from blemishes. Photographs can be retouched to remove blemishes, or to improve contrast or detail. However, this is expensive, and where scanners are used, sometimes the retouching marks will show up on the final result. Any retouching should be discussed with the color house before reproduction.

Black and white halftone originals can be reproduced in four color to give more depth and detail, although this is more expensive (see pages 86–87).

Sizing and cropping are done as for line.

COLOR FLAT ARTWORK The presentation of color flat artwork is described in detail on page 42. Very large originals may be too big to fit around the drum of the scanner, and the designer may need to have a transparency made.

SPECIAL COLORS AND TINTS These can present particular problems (see pages 44–45).

IDENTIFYING ORIGINALS All originals should carry a figure number and page number (if known). The separation house can then be asked to put these numbers on the film and proofs of each subject, to assist the identification of subjects. This is particularly important on large jobs that are scatter-proofed.

INSURANCE Many transparencies are valued by the photographer at around $660 (£400) and some at as much as $3,300 (£2,000). It is normally the client's responsibility to insure originals against loss or damage occurring either at the design studio or the color separation house, or in transit. It is worthwhile checking the insurance cover with both the client and the color house. If a color house loses or damages an original, it will normally offer some compensation, but not necessarily to the same value as that put on it by the photographer or artist.

CHECKING MATERIAL

Keep a checklist of all the originals by figure and/or page number and give totals for the different types of originals (transparencies, color flat artworks, black and white halftone originals etc.).

The list should accompany the originals to the repro house and the originals should be checked against it when returned. Report

Reproduction techniques
Lithography and other processes

EFFECTIVE CORRECTION of color proofs demands at least a basic knowledge of reproduction techniques, in order that the designer can understand the possibilities and limitations of the separation and printing process.

Offset lithography is the process used for the majority of work handled by designers, and this section deals with reproduction by this process.

LINE ORIGINATION The original, which is normally black and white, is placed on the copy board of a graphic arts camera. The graphic arts camera is a very large version of an ordinary camera and works in a similar way to the PMT (photomechanical transfer) machines used by designers. Film coated with a light-sensitive emulsion is placed in the back of the camera, behind the lens. The original is lit with a bright light and the shutter of the camera opened to expose the image on the film.

On exposure, light reflected from the white area of the original passes through the lens to fall on the film emulsion, which contains silver halide, which responds to light and blackens during development. When the film has been developed to produce a negative, unexposed silver, which will not have blackened, is dissolved in a fixing solution. The negative can be used for platemaking or contact printed to make a positive in cases where plates need positives rather than negatives, normally for color work.

The size of the image is determined by adjusting the lens and the copy board on the camera, and the exposure is timed to ensure that the film image is neither underexposed ("thick") nor overexposed ("thin").

Typeset material is treated as a line original when supplied in the form of CRC and is shot on a camera in the same way. In some cases the filmsetting machine can produce a negative or positive and this makes it unnecessary for the type to be shot.

HALFTONE ORIGINATION A continuous-tone original, such as a black and white photograph, cannot be shot as line, as the different shades of gray will not be picked up by the camera. This type of original has to be reproduced as a halftone.

The different shades of gray in a black and white photograph cannot be printed in gray, for in this case

Nearly all color separation is now done on scanners like this. Scanning has replaced separation on camera and is faster, less expensive, and gives much more control. Scanners can be linked to other electronic equipment to produce complete made-up pages.

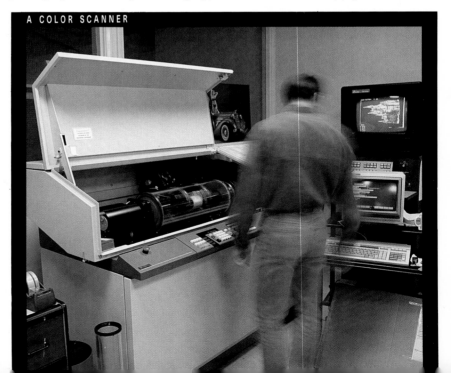

A COLOR SCANNER

the printing press uses only black ink. The halftone process therefore simulates the grays by breaking the picture up into small dots. These are largest in the dark areas and smallest in the pale areas. When printed, this arrangement gives the effect of the different shades of gray, even though only black ink has been used.

Halftones can be reproduced on graphic arts cameras, although now most are scanned. In the case of camera reproduction, the halftone effect is achieved by placing a screen in the back of the camera between the lens and the film. The screen, made of film, has a grid of fine lines which breaks the image up into dots, producing a halftone negative. In black and white reproduction, the halftone screen is normally placed at an angle of 45° to the horizontal, as this makes the rows of dots less obvious to the eye.

Another camera technique used for halftones is to produce a continuous-tone negative on the graphic arts camera and place a contact screen between the negative and a sheet of unexposed film, which becomes a screened positive on exposure.

Screens can be coarse or fine; screen rulings are described in detail on pages 50-51.

Halftones can also be produced as PMTs. A PMT is a screened halftone print on photographic paper, and designers with PMT machines can produce these in the studio. Because the PMT is already screened, it can be pasted into CRC and the whole paste-up can then be photographed as a line shot. This saves the expense of shooting the photographs onto film and stripping them in at the film stage.

However, screened PMTs cannot give first-rate quality and should probably not be used finer than 120 screen. Therefore the designer must be discriminating in the type of job for which PMTs are used.

The majority of pencil drawings are treated as halftones in order to reproduce the subtle shades of

A graphic arts camera is used to reproduce black and white line illustrations and halftones. In shooting halftones a screen is used to break the picture up into dots.

Black and white scanners are now widely used, leaving the camera just to shoot type and line work.

gray, which cannot be achieved in line origination. The background can be dropped out so that it carries no dot pattern, but is just white paper.

SCANNING HALFTONES Until fairly recently, most halftones were reproduced on cameras, since scanners were available only for four-color process work. However, a new generation of monochrome scanners has meant that the majority of halftone work is now scanned. A scanner's end product is a screened positive, as with a camera, but as this is produced by electronic means there is much more control over the process, resulting in much better quality. It is also cheaper and there is a higher productivity. The scanning of black and white halftones uses the same basic principles as scanning color (see page 14).

The characteristics of good black and white halftone originals and reproductions are discussed on pages 82-83. Sometimes black and white photo-

To separate color originals the halftone principle is used in the same way as for black and white photographs. Each color film is made up of dots of sizes that differ according to the density of color in the corresponding area of the original. A normal 133-screen image (above) is shown enlarged 400% (below).

Dots of the four process colors enlarged are shown right.

To avoid screen clash, or moiré, the screen lines are set at different angles to each other.

YELLOW

YELLOW MAGENTA

YELLOW MAGENTA CYAN

YELLOW MAGENTA CYAN BLACK

graphs are reproduced by the four-color process to give more depth (see pages 86–87). These are scanned in exactly the same way as four-color sets.

DUOTONES A duotone is a two-color halftone (see pages 84–85). It can be produced on a camera or scanner as described above, but two negatives are produced, rather than one.

LINE AND TONE A combination of line and halftone is a negative contacted from two films – one line and the other halftone. The process is used, for example, where solid type is to appear superimposed on a photograph.

COLOR SEPARATION Color originals must be "separated" so that the effect of full color can be achieved by printing in only four colors. This is done by breaking down the original into three colors – magenta, cyan, and yellow, to which black is added to give finer detail and add density to dark areas.

Known as the "four-color process," this operation results in four pieces of film. It is possible to reproduce most colors from combinations of two or more of these four colors. For example, a purple is produced by putting a certain amount of magenta with a certain amount of cyan, the proportions varying according to the particular shade required.

However, certain colors are impossible to produce accurately with the four-color process (see pages 44–45).

SCANNING Described above is the basic separation process as done on a camera, but nearly all separation is now carried out on scanners. The same separation principles apply, but the scanner uses a high-intensity light or laser beam to scan the original and separate the colors. The color filters and a computer are built into the scanner and convert the signals picked up by the beam into screened posi-

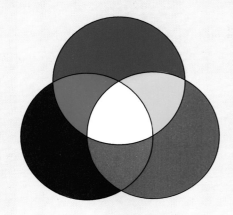

"White" light is a combination of all the colors of the spectrum. These can be broken down into three "primary" colors – red, green, and blue. Since these three colors when added together, make white light, they are known as the "additive" primaries (above). When one is taken away, the other two combined make a different color. Red and blue produce magenta, while green and blue give cyan. Magenta, cyan, and yellow are "subtractive" primaries or "secondary" colors (below).

In printing, the four process colors are the three subtractive primaries – magenta, cyan, and yellow – and black. To make a film that will produce the required color, a filter of the respective additive primary color is used (right). For example, to make a negative film for the yellow, a blue filter is used. This absorbs all the wavelengths of light reflected from the yellow components of the original, so that yellow is not recorded on the emulsion. When developed, the "black" part of the negative will represent everything in the original that is not yellow, and the clear part therefore includes all the yellow components of the original. Similarly, a green filter will produce a negative for the magenta and a red filter a negative for the cyan.

red filter   green filter   blue filter

negative   red   green   blue

positive   cyan   magenta   yellow

three positives combined to make all colors

black added

final four-color reproduction

tives for each of the four colors.

Compared to a process camera, the scanner is much faster and gives superior quality, and most modern scanners can separate all four colors at once. The scanner operator has access to a range of sophisticated electronic controls which can achieve a faithfulness to the original that with camera separation could be achieved only by retouching the separated film.

If a job has originals that are to be reduced or enlarged by the same percentage, these can be scanned together, saving cost. These originals are described as "in pro" (in proportion). However, in addition to the same reduction or enlargement, the originals must also have similar density ranges, otherwise the scanner settings that suit one original will not give a good result with another. In such cases it can be left to the separation house to decide what to do.

The originals are taped to the drum of the scanner, and the scanner operator sets the percentage enlargement or reduction and the screen ruling. A densitometer is used to take readings of the density of colors in different parts of the original, and then the scanner is set up accordingly.

The scanner drum holding the original rotates at high speed, and the scanning head analyzes the image as it moves along the drum. The signals are sent via the color filters to the computer, which converts the digital information into light signals that are exposed on film.

Color flat artwork is scanned in the same way, but must be on flexible board so that it can be wrapped around the drum. Color artwork can contain strong hues which are difficult to reproduce in four colors.

Most modern scanners use a laser beam and produce a hard dot (see page 60) which limits the amount of hand retouching.

While most scanners use rotating drums for inputting scanned images, some now use a flat bed system. Usually these are mono scanners – that is, only for black and white. However, some color separation houses do offer a flat bed system which will take color transparencies or flat artwork, though no bigger than 8 × 10in (20 × 25cm).

The best-known manufacturers of scanners are Crosfield, Hell, Dai Nippon, and Itek. Each makes several different models with different features and capable of taking a variety of sizes of originals.

ELECTRONIC PAGE MAKE-UP Now in common use, electronic page make-up systems can scan, store

For small-scale scanning the transparency is fixed to the drum with either an adhesive lacquer (below) or tape (inset).

PREPARING TO SCAN

MAKING BIG ENLARGEMENTS

When a big enlargement is required, the surface is covered with oil to minimize the effects of surface scratches (left). The oil is held in place by clear plastic foil (inset).

the separation information on a hard disk in digital form, and then use it to create complete pages with several transparencies, tints, and rules. The resulting page films are one-piece films for each color. In addition, electronic page make-up systems can produce shapes and cut-outs, do airbrushing and vignetting and carry out color correction.

Most of these systems have a color monitor, enabling the operator to check everything before it is committed to film. Some systems can include type as well as pictures in the layout and can even alter typefaces and type sizes at layout stage.

These systems are very costly, but their sophistication enables color houses to produce complex publications such as mail order catalogues more economically and with better results. Besides these complete systems, there are also independent work stations which can interface with the scanner.

Nearly all these systems are installed in color separation houses rather than design studios. However, designers in some larger magazine companies are now turning to electronic page make-up. The advantage is that the design is done in "real time." This means that when the designer changes the size of an image the operation is carried out there and then, rather than a design decision being enacted by the color house at a later stage.

DESKTOP PUBLISHING Until recently, desktop publishing (DTP) has been used mainly for typesetting work with line illustration and simple black and white halftones. However, there is now a blurring of the distinction between DTP and electronic page make-up. DTP allows the designer to design a page of typesetting, pictures in black and white and color, as well as tints/rules, etc. and end up with a disk containing all this information, which can be sent to the color house for outputting onto film.

CAD DRAFTING AND MASKING SYSTEMS Computer systems perform some of the functions of electronic page make-up systems, such as tint laying, drafting and masking, but are much cheaper than the full systems.

TINTS Where the designer requires a flat area of color, the separation normally produces it by using tints. A tint is not solid ink, but is made up from dots of the four process colors. The colors are screened in percentages, usually in increments of 10%, and a tint may consist of one process color or be combined with one or more of the other three colors. This yields a possible 1,400 combinations.

When a special color is to be matched by using the four-color process, it is always better to specify the

After scanning, the film is developed and fixed in a film processor (below). Shown here the final piece of film for one of the four process colors (inset).

SCANNING

The drum holding the original rotates at high speed (left). The panel below has the control keys for color density and sizing. The monitor (inset) analyzes the image and converts it into digital signals.

PROCESSING FILM

percentages of different colors as above, rather than give a color swatch or PANTONE®★ reference and ask the color house to match it. Some special colors cannot be exactly matched from the process, and rather than find this out at proof stage, it is better to specify a tint knowing that the color house will be able to match it (see pages 44-45).

DOT GAIN Describes the increase in size of the dot from film dot to printed dot (see pages 62-63).

UNDERCOLOR REMOVAL This and achromatic reproduction are explained on pages 46-47.

PROOFING Once film has been made, a proof is produced so that the client, designer, and color house can check the quality, sizing, and positioning. The printer will also require a proof to match when printing the job.

Where jobs are varnished, laminated, or foil blocked, or have some other kind of special finish, the color house can usually send the proofs to the finishing supplier to have the operation carried out,

so that the proof has all the characteristics of the finished job. However, these finishing operations can usually be carried out only on wet proofs on paper, as the photographic material used in Cromalins and Matchprints cannot be laminated, varnished, or foil blocked. Note also that in order to block, a mold will have to be made and artwork supplied for this at the same time as the other originals.

CHECKING COLOR PROOFS The checking of color proofs is dealt with in detail on page 80.

PASSING COLOR ON MACHINE The question on page 141 describes how to check color at the printing stage.

FILM ASSEMBLY This term describes the assembly of all the type and pictorial elements within a page in the correct position. In most cases, the typesetter or designer will already have positioned the type in page form as camera-ready copy, leaving spaces for any illustrations. The color house will shoot the CRC (see page 12) and make negative or positive film from it.

If the color house is to produce scatter proofs (see pages 56-57) and random film, the assembly will be done by the printer at the same time as imposition.

IMPOSITION This is the placing of the pages in the correct position on the plate so that in the finished job they come out in the right order and with the correct margins.

A typical electronic page make-up system consists of a color monitor, a keyboard, and a "mouse." The operator manipulates the images and type to fit the designer's layout (below).

When checked, page film is produced on the output scanner. This avoids all the handwork involved in combining the different elements using conventional reproduction techniques.

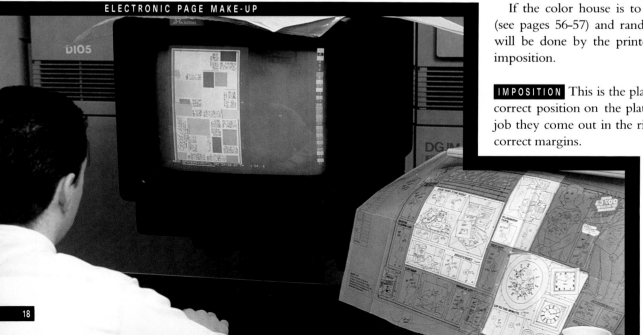

ELECTRONIC PAGE MAKE-UP

*Pantone, Inc's check standard trademark for color reproduction and color reproduction materials.

Most presses print 8, 16, or 32 pages (or multiples of these) to view (on one side of the paper) and the printer works out an imposition scheme that will print the required number of pages in the most economical way on the press being used. The designer will not normally need to know the details of the imposition unless part of the job is being printed in a different number of colors (e.g. four colors backing two). Here the designer will need to get the imposition scheme from the printer, to establish which pages are printed in the different ways. The illustrations and layout can then be planned according to which pages are printed in four colors and which in two.

The imposition itself is normally done with Scotch tape on clear plastic foils, which are positioned on top of the layout grid. This is a slow and expensive hand operation, and some printers now use electronic imposition systems, such as Opticopy or Rachwal.

The Opticopy is basically a camera which holds a very large piece of film the same size as the printing plate. The pages are photographed one at a time, and the machine moves the film each time, exposing each page in the correct position for printing. The operation is controlled by a computer with different programs for the required imposition schemes.

The Rachwal system photographs each page onto a reel of 70mm film. This is then put into a projection head which enlarges the page to full size and exposes it directly onto the printing plate.

Another machine that automates imposition is the "step and repeat" machine. This has a projection head containing negative or positive film, which is moved automatically under computer control and exposes the image onto the plate each time it moves. This machine is used particularly for making plates that have multiple copies of the same image. For example, it is used a lot in packaging, where a small carton might be printed with 32 or more of the same image on the plate.

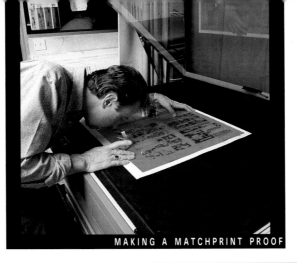

MAKING A MATCHPRINT PROOF

The magenta film is being placed over the red laminate before exposure (left). The process is repeated for the other three colors.

The yellow laminate being applied to the base sheet after the cyan and magenta have been processed (right).

The color bar for the yellow is being placed in contact with the yellow laminate (left). The color bar will show not only the density of color being used, but also dot gain and other characteristics of the proof.

Printing processes
Offset lithography • Letterpress • Gravure • Screen printing • Foil blocking • Embossing

THE MAIN PRINTING PROCESS used now is offset lithography, on which this chapter will concentrate. However, from time to time designers will deal with work produced by the other processes, such as letterpress, flexography, gravure, or screen printing.

The printing surfaces used by letterpress, lithography, and gravure have different physical characteristics. Letterpress is a "relief" process in which the image to be printed is raised above the background. This raised surface is inked by rollers and then pressed against the paper to make the impression. Lithography is "planographic"; that is, using a flat printing surface. The image area is chemically treated so that it accepts ink and rejects

water, while the non-image area is treated to accept water and reject ink. Gravure is an "intaglio" process, in which the printing image is recessed into the plate and filled with liquid ink. The non-image area is wiped free of ink, so the ink is deposited on the paper from the recessed cells only.

OFFSET LITHOGRAPHY This is the predominant printing process, being used for a wide range of items from stationery to books and magazines. Lithography was invented by Aloïs Senefelder in Bavaria in 1798, but it was only when the offset principle was applied early in the present century that lithography started to be used for commercial (as opposed to art) printing. It was as recently as the

---

THE LITHOGRAPHY PROCESS

Lithography has a planographic (flat) printing surface. The image area accepts ink and repels water. The non-image area repels ink and attracts water. The four diagrams on the right show the original lithographic process, which printed directly onto paper. Nearly all lithographic printing is now done by offset lithography (or "offset"), which is shown on the opposite page.

The image area of the plate is first treated with a greasy medium and then dampened with water by rollers.

The plate is inked by rollers, the ink adhering to the greasy image but not to the dampened areas.

The paper is pressed against the plate.

Advantages

Good reproduction of detail and photographs
Inexpensive printing surface
Fast make-ready
Rubber blanket enables use of wide range of papers
Lends itself to photographic reproduction methods
Rotary principle allows higher printing speeds

Disadvantages

Color variation due to problems with ink/water balance
Dampening can cause paper stretch
Dense film of ink difficult to achieve

OFFSET LITHOGRAPHY

water and reject grease (ink). The surface of the printing plate has both water and ink applied to it. When the inked and dampened plate is pressed against the paper, only the image area is printed.

Lithographic printing was first done using smooth stone slabs as the printing surface, and this method is still used by artists to make original lithographic prints. Modern offset lithography uses plates made of grained aluminum.

The offset press The offset press carries out the operations of feeding, damping (applying water to the plate), inking, printing, and delivering the finished sheet.

The system uses the rotary principle, in which the press acts somewhat like a mangle, with the cylinders rolling against each other. The printing section of the press consists of three cylinders – a blanket cylinder around which a sheet of rubber is wrapped, a plate cylinder carrying the printing plate, and the impression cylinder which presses the paper against the blanket to make the impression.

1960s that the offset lithography process began gradually to overtake letterpress.

In lithography (litho) the printing surface is flat rather than raised, as in letterpress, or recessed, as in gravure. The area to be printed is treated chemically so that it accepts grease (ink) and rejects water, while the non-image (background) area is treated to accept

The final printed image.

In offset printing the inked image on the metal plate is offset (printed) onto a rubber blanket wrapped round a rotating metal cylinder and the image is then transferred from the blanket to the paper. The reason for printing via the blanket rather than directly from plate onto paper is that the plate's surface is delicate.

If the plate came into contact with the abrasive paper surface, rapid wear on the plate would occur.

Another advantage of the offset principle is that less water comes

impression cylinder

blanket cylinder

plate cylinder

into contact with the paper, so avoiding problems of paper shrinkage which would give rise to register (positioning) problems. Also, being slightly elastic, the rubber blanket responds to surface irregularities, so that it is possible to print on a wide variety of surfaces.

Letterpress is a "relief" process—that is, the printing surface holding the image to be printed is raised above the non-printing background. The raised surface is inked by rollers and then pressed against the paper to make the impression. The background does not print because, being lower than the printing area, it does not come into contact with either the inking rollers or the paper.

In traditional letterpress, all the text is printed from metal type and the pictures from letterpress cuts. These elements are assembled together (imposed) to make a "form" inside a rigid frame or "chase," which is placed in the press. The printing surface is therefore made up of hundreds or thousands of different pieces of type, cuts, and spacing (left).

The image area of a letterpress block or piece of type is raised, while the non-image areas are recessed so that they do not pick up ink.

The surface is inked by a roller.

Sheet-fed offset Sheet-fed offset presses range from the small machines used in instant print shops which print 8½ × 11 size, up to large book presses which can print 35 × 45 size. They may print only one color or up to six colors. Some machines (called "perfecting presses") can print both sides of the sheet in one operation.

Most multi-color presses print four colors and are used for four-color process work (printing black, cyan, yellow, and magenta).

Web-fed offset Most web-offset presses are "blanket-to-blanket"; that is, the web of paper runs between the two blanket cylinders so that both sides are printed simultaneously, with each of the blanket cylinders acting as the impression cylinder to the other.

Many web-offset presses are designed to print an 8½ × 11 product, as this is the size of most magazines and catalogues. These presses print 16, 32, or 64 pages at a time.

Web-offset machines fold the paper as they print, and, with high printing speeds, this means that where color is being printed, the ink has to be dried before folding to prevent "set-off" (smudging). The drying is done by passing the printed web of paper through a tunnel before folding. There are several methods of drying; these include gas-flame, hot air, ultra-violet and infra-red.

Despite their high speed, web-offset presses can produce good quality. In fact, the drying facility on web presses means that a thicker film of ink can be carried than on sheet-fed presses, giving more depth and gloss. Also, many web presses can give extra gloss by the use of a silicone applicator after printing.

Web-offset machines are used to print magazines, travel brochures, some books, mail-order catalogues and long-run (30,000-plus) brochures. Many newspapers, both local and national, have switched in recent years from letterpress to web-offset, which gives better quality reproduction of photographs, offers color, and links more readily with modern typesetting methods.

Paper is placed over the inked image and pressed onto it by an impression cylinder.

The final printed image.

A letterpress cut is made by photosensitizing a piece of copper or zinc and exposing it under a negative. The image area that is clear on the negative is hardened by the light and therefore becomes resistant to corrosion by acid. When the plate is etched, the acid etches the non-image area to below the image area so that it does not print.

Letterpress cuts can be made for four-color process printing from negatives separated on cameras or scanners as for offset lithography.

LETTERPRESS Letterpress was overtaken in the 1960s and eventually replaced as the main printing process by offset. The reasons for this include the high cost of metal type and cuts; the greater cost of the papers required to give a good result; the relatively slow speed of most letterpress machines; and the fact that modern methods of reproduction (for both text and pictures) do not lend themselves to the creation of a raised surface.

However, there are still several areas in which letterpress is used successfully. These include private-press work (from metal type), business forms, labels, and computer stationery.

Letterpress presses The platen press is used for small jobs (maximum size 11 × 17) and consists of two flat surfaces of metal, hinged at the bottom, which are brought together under pressure to make the impression. The form with the type and cuts is fixed onto one surface and inked by rollers, and the paper is placed on the other surface. The platen press can be used for small "jobbing" work such as letterheads, tickets, and small leaflets, although most of this work is now done on small offset presses. Platen presses are, however, still used for embossing, cutting and creasing, and hot-foil blocking.

The flat-bed cylinder press holds the form in a flat metal bed while the ink rollers and sheets of

---

LETTERPRESS

Advantages
Dense ink
Good printing of type for high-quality books
No problems with ink/water balance
Less paper wastage than other processes

Disadvantages
High cost of printing surface
More expensive paper needed to get same results as other processes
Sheet-fed machines run slowly
Modern reproduction methods suit other processes better

paper roll over it alternately. The paper is held around a cylinder while it is pressed on the form to make the impression. At one time most books and magazines were printed on this type of press. Nowadays, they are used by private presses for high-quality limited edition book work.

The rotary press prints from a curved or flexible metal or plastic plate, which is clamped on a cylinder which revolves against another cylinder carrying the paper. Rotary presses can be sheet-fed or web-fed, and where letterpress is still used, it is mainly now on rotary presses.

GRAVURE Before the invention of modern gravure methods, artists had used a similar method of printing to produce etchings, in which the image was etched into a copper plate, filled with ink, and printed on flat-bed presses. The introduction of photogravure (also known as rotogravure) dates from the use of photographic methods, in which the printing surface is produced from film.

Gravure is an "intaglio" process; that is, the printing image is recessed into the plate, rather than being flat (as in lithography) or raised (as in letterpress). The image consists of cells engraved into a copper-plated plate or cylinder. These cells are filled with liquid ink, and the cells vary in depth so that they will leave the required amount of ink on the various parts of the printed image. A blade (known as a doctor blade) is pulled across the surface of the plate or cylinder to remove excess ink. The paper is fed through the press on an electrostatic rubber-covered cylinder which presses the paper into the recesses to pick up the ink.

The ink is very thin and, being spirit-based, dries through evaporation immediately after printing. Unlike web-offset, therefore, the process does not need elaborate drying arrangements.

The gravure press Most gravure printing is done on web-fed machines, using rolls of paper and folding on press. The machines are usually very large, printing up to 128 pages of $8\frac{1}{2} \times 11$ size and running at speeds of up to 50,000 an hour. Sheet-fed gravure presses are used for stamps and very high quality photographic books, but there are very few

---

THE GRAVURE PROCESS

Gravure is an intaglio process, which means that the printing image is recessed into the plate and filled with ink. The cells vary in depth but not in size (left).

Because of the cell structure, type can look fuzzy in smaller sizes, as the cell walls break up the fine detail. Yet gravure printing of photographs is often superior to other processes, as it gives a true "halftone" effect in which the darker areas of the photograph actually carry more ink as they are printed from deeper cells.

Photographs printed by gravure have greater contrast between light and dark areas, as a heavy film of ink is carried. Gravure can also give good results on quite cheap papers.

The reason why gravure is mainly used for very long runs is that the plates and cylinders are very expensive to buy and prepare and this high start-up cost can be recovered only from a long run.

The printing image is recessed and ink is applied by a roller. It fills the cells and some remains on the surface.

A thin, flexible steel blade (a doctor blade) is drawn across the plate to remove excess ink from the non-printing areas.

Advantages

Simple printing method and press mechanism
Can maintain consistent color
High speed
Straightforward drying by evaporation
Good results obtainable on inexpensive and
lightweight paper

Disadvantages

High cost of plates and cylinders
Viable only for long runs (300,000-plus)
Color correction and last-minute corrections
difficult and expensive
Proofing expensive

GRAVURE

of these presses still running.

Uses of gravure Gravure is used for very long-run (300,000 copies or more) magazines (such as newspaper color magazines) and mail order catalogues. It is also used for some kinds of packaging, printing on cellophane, decorative laminates, and wallpaper.

SCREEN PRINTING In screen printing, a stencil cut by hand or made photographically (see pages 20–21) is supported on a screen of synthetic fiber or metal. In the early days of the process, the screen was made of silk and the process known as silk-screen printing.

The screen is stretched over a frame of wood or metal, and ink is spread along the screen by means of a rubber squeegee, which squeezes the ink through the screen in the image areas. The stencil prevents ink from going through in the non-image (background) areas.

The screen-printing press Many screen presses are manually operated, in both the feeding of the paper and the application of the ink. These presses consist of a simple frame hinged to a flat surface. The advantage of this type of equipment is that it is very cheap and so lends itself to printing at home, or the printing of posters by community groups. Artists can also produce original prints on this type of equipment.

In semi-automatic presses, the screen is raised and lowered automatically and the squeegee operation is also automatic, but the paper or other material to be

The paper is put on the plate and pressed against it by a roller. The pressure forces the paper into the cells to pick up the ink.

The final printed image.

In the "litho-to-gravure" conversion technique, proofs are produced as for litho and can be Matchprints or Cromalins or wet proofs. The designer corrects these in exactly the same way as litho proofs and the color house carries out the corrections before making the opalines. It is expensive to correct the cylinders once made, but it can be done by chemical methods. The chemicals etch the cells to make them deeper to give stronger color, or fill them in to make them shallower and give

weaker color. The latter is more difficult.

Gravure is a specialized process, and even more than in litho, it is important for the designer to work closely with the color house and printer, as techniques of gravure reproduction and printing can vary from one supplier to another much more than in the relatively standardized litho process.

Litho-to-gravure proofs always look a little flatter, as the conversion entails some loss of highlights.

Regardless of the printing process used, the paper can be fed into the press either as sheets or as rolls of paper. When paper is made it comes off the papermaking machine in very large rolls. Where printing is to be sheet-fed, this paper is slit on the roll and then cut up into sheets of the required size. The feeder on the press picks up the sheets with a combination of metal fingers and vacuum suckers

and feeds them through to be printed. After printing, the flat sheets are folded on a separate machine.

In web-fed printing, the paper is supplied to the machine in the form of rolls. These can be as wide as 13ft (4m) on some presses. The front end of the press has a roll stand, which holds the paper as it is unwound and fed through the press. The method of making the impression is the same as with a sheet-fed press, but the web-fed press runs much faster because the machine is not slowed down by having to pick up and put down each sheet. Most web presses can fold on press and some can also glue, perforate, or wire-stitch.

The advantages of web-fed printing are: speed (15,000 to 40,000 impressions per hour compared with 5,000 to 12,000 for sheet-fed printing); the fact that folding can be done as an in-line operation; and economy – savings can be made by buying paper in rolls rather than sheets. The disadvantages are that web-fed machines have a much higher capital cost and a longer make-ready time (see opposite) and most machines can produce only items of a fixed length. Also, web-fed presses waste more paper than sheet-fed, during both make-ready and running, due to the higher speed.

printed is inserted and removed by hand.

Screen-printing machines often have vacuum bases to help separate the paper from the screen after printing. Fully automatic presses also feed and deliver the stock automatically, and some have an impression cylinder which holds the paper while the screen moves in unison and the squeegee remains stationary. Automatic presses can print at up to 6,000 impressions an hour.

Because of the thick film of ink used, drying can be a problem, and on short runs the sheets are laid out to dry on racks. However, it is quite common for automatic machines to have drying tunnels or ultra-violet drying units.

Uses of screen printing Because the process can apply a thick layer of ink and print large sheets of paper, it is ideal for posters. The screen process can print on virtually any material including wood, fabric, glass, plastic and metal. Screen printing is the process used for plastic and metal signs, bottles, transfers, and printed circuits. It can also print on very light papers, such as sewing patterns, which would cause feeding problems in other processes.

FLEXOGRAPHY This is a derivative of the letterpress process, using flexible relief plates and thin, fluid inks that dry by evaporation (sometimes assisted by heat). The plates are made from either rubber or photopolymer with the image raised as in conventional letterpress.

The flexographic press Most presses for flexography are web-fed. Ink is applied to the plate by a metal "anilox" roller with cells etched into it, which carry the ink and transfer it to the plate. Machines can be multi-color for four-color process work.

Uses of flexography Flexography is mainly used for packaging (see pages 134–137) – printing on cellophane, plastic, and metallic foils. It can in fact be used for virtually any material that will physically pass through the press. It is also used for some local

---

SCREEN PRINTING

Advantages
Can print a heavy film of ink
Economical for short runs (even below 100 copies)
Can print on virtually any material

Disadvantages
Difficult to achieve fine detail
Low output
Drying requirements

and national newspapers, although offset is gaining ground in this field because it reproduces black and white and color photographs better and makes type sharper.

Although most mass-market paperback books are printed offset, some suppliers still successfully print by flexography, using photopolymer plates.

Flexography used to be the poor relation of the other processes, but improvements in plates and inks are ensuring its growth.

FOIL BLOCKING AND EMBOSSING Although not strictly speaking a printing process, because it forms part of the binding or finishing operation, foil blocking is in common use on promotional items of print and book covers and jackets.

Blocking and embossing are done on converted letterpress machines of either the platen or flat-bed type, and the image is carried on a brass which has a raised surface and is made in the same way as a letterpress cut (see page 25). The brass is fixed on the bed or platen, which is heated, and then the brass is pressed into a ribbon of foil. The combination of heat and pressure detaches the metallic foil from its carrier ribbon and applies it to the paper, creating a three-dimensional effect at the same time. "Blind" embossing is done in very much the same manner, but without the use of foil.

Because blocking and embossing are fairly crude

processes, the designer should not attempt to use too much fine detail or small type, as it may well get squashed. Simple designs and bold type work best. Finally, you should bear in mind that finishing can extend the schedule.

MAKE-READY In all printing processes make-ready must be carried out before printing can begin. The operation includes setting up the press to accept the size and thickness of paper being used, putting the printing plates on, changing the ink if necessary, adjusting the folder (on a web-fed press), and ensuring that the color is the right strength and that the image is in the correct position.

Make-ready is important because good quality depends on it. Also, because presses are not producing while making ready, make-ready forms an important part of the cost of printing.

Rubber duplicate plates (below) for printing a paperback book by flexography. Each page is a separate rubber plate and is fixed with adhesive to a plastic foil base.

A photopolymer plate (right). A flexible plate for printing by letterpress or flexography, it is made photographically from a negative. The image area is in relief.

29

ALL ABOUT

PROOFS

This section explains the basic principles of how originals are presented to the color separation house and what the four-color process can achieve. Paper, dot gain, undercolor removal, and moiré are all explained in detail.

The different methods of proofing are shown, as well as how the color house produces final film and carries out corrections.

What do I need to tell the color house

ONCE THE DESIGN of a job has been completed, it takes the work of the color house and printer to bring it to a successful conclusion. It is absolutely vital that there be good communication between the three parties at this stage, rather than each working independently.

In some cases, one company will carry out both

the rep...
can saf...
internal...
and prin...
and it is u...
to ensure...
of the oth... If this is not done, the result could be a job on which the proofs look excellent, but where it is impossible to obtain the same result on the final printed work.

The main means of communicating the required information is the printer's specification sheet. This tells the color house what the printer requires as regards: screen ruling, paper type, dot shape, dot gain, ink densities, minimum and maximum dot sizes, undercolor removal (if required), type of color bar.

Other information that the printer might give includes: imposition sheets (showing trims and bleeds), imposition scheme (showing where pages fall), plate specifications (if the color house is supplying plates rather than film), type of film (negative or positive and right-reading or wrong-reading when viewed with the emulsion side down).

In addition to the specification sheet, if a job poses particular problems, it is a good idea for the designer to set up a meeting with the color house and printer to look at the layouts and originals, before repro-duction starts.

The color house should be advised if the job is to be varnished or laminated.

PRINTER'S SPECIFICATION SHEET

On specification sheets, check the dot gain and ink densities. These can vary from one printer to another, as can the proofing sequence.

A PRINTER

Reproduction requirements for sheet-fed offset

COLOR BAR   Gretag CMS2 control strip

DENSITOMETER   Gretag

DENSITY READINGS	COLOR	DENSITY	TOL.	80% DOT GAIN	TOL.	40% DOT GAIN	TOL.
GLOSS COATED PAPER	CYAN	1.45	±0.10	9	±2	14	±3
	MAGENTA	1.40	±0.10	9	±2	14	±3
	YELLOW	1.40	±0.10	10	±2	16	±3
	BLACK	1.85	±0.15	10	±2	16	±3
MATTE COATED	CYAN	1.35	±0.10	10	±3	15	±4
	MAGENTA	1.30	±0.10	10	±3	15	±4
	YELLOW	1.30	±0.10	11	±3	17	±4
	BLACK	1.75	±0.15	11	±3	17	±4
UNCOATED	CYAN	1.20	±0.10	14	±4	21	±5
	MAGENTA	1.15	±0.10	14	±4	21	±5
	YELLOW	1.20	±0.10	14	±4	21	±5
	BLACK	1.55	±0.15	15	±4	22	±5

PROOFING SEQUENCE – Cyan, Magenta, Yellow, Black

DOT SHAPE – Elliptic

PERCENTAGE OF UNDERCOLOR REMOVAL – CYAN   85%
                                                                    – MAGENTA 75%
                                                                    – YELLOW   75%
                                                                    – BLACK   95%

SCREEN RULING – 150

FILM – Positive film right-reading emulsion-down. 4 thou thick

```
                                    Op
                40253a
L000
  Spec-check
  FACE
  DPS: Overall gutter loss - 10mm
  Pub.Co.:  Wagadon Ltd
  Address:  The Old Laundry
  (Copy)    Ossington Buildings
            Off Moxon Street
            LONDON W1

  Contact:  Rod Sopp
  Tel:      01-935 8232
  Page  Type:   283 x 212      DPS: 283 x 444
  Page Bleed:   313 x 242      DPS: 313 x 474
  Page  Trim:   303 x 232      DPS: 303 x 464
  Half  Type:   281 x 102 or 138 x 210
  Half Bleed:        x      or      x        or
  Half  Trim:        x      or      x        x
  Qtr   Page:   138 x 102 or    Mini:   x

  Display Cols:           Length:    ,    ,
    Col Widths:       ',   Length:
  Class.  Cols:          ,
    Col Widths:     ',   9 Spec-check Index
  £ to continue...
```

```
                                    Op
                40253b
L000
  Spec-check
  THE FACE
  Printed: Web Offset
  Binding: Perfect     Cvrs-135gsm
  Paper Wght: Text-80gsm    C-Kaukas
       Make: T-Kaukas
  Publ.Date: Monthly 3/4th Thurs prec.
  Display copy dates:-
  Mech + Trans B&W- 3 weeks Col- 3 weeks
  Final Film  B&W- 3 weeks Col- 3 weeks
  Class. copy dates:-
             B&W- n/a
  Printer: Severn Valley Printers
  Nearest Red Star: Cardiff

  Copy Required:-
  B&W:     Bromides/Artwork + Cont Tone/
           Film: Positives RRE Down
  Colour:  Artwork + Transparencies/
           Film: Positives RRE Down
  Screen Size:   48 B&W    54 Colour
  Method Of Punching: n/a
  £ to continue           9 Spec-check Index
```

```
                                    Op
                40253c
L000
  Spec-check
  THE FACE
                  Y      C      M      B
  Screen Angles:  90     75     45     15
  Density:        1.1    1.3    1.3    1.8
  Dot Gain: 18% in 40%,  14% in 75%
  UCR: Between 200% and 270%
  Proofing Method: n/a
  No. Of Proofs Required: n/a
  Colour Sequence: n/a
  Proof Direction: n/a

  Special Instructions:

  Inserts:-
  - Loose: Size       )  Available on
           Weight     )  Application
  - Bound: Size       )
           Weight     )
           Guard Width )
                          9 Spec-check Index
```

Color specification sheet (left) for *The Face*

RRE This means that the film supplied by the printer will be positive. RRE stands for Right Reading Emulsion down. Sometimes a spec will state WRE, which means Wrong Reading Emulsion down. Whether RRE or WRE is chosen depends on the printing process.

Density These figures represent the ink densities at which the printer runs its press to give the optimum results. Ink densities vary depending on what is being printed – for example a newspaper would be printed on .7 for all colors.

UCR This stands for undercolor removal. The range of figures given here represents the combined percentages of the four colors with UCR. If the printer specifies a maximum of 270% the individual percentages of each color will be: cyan 65% + yellow 55% + magenta 55% + black 95% = 270% maximum.

Screen angles This part of the spec shows the angle for each color used by the printer.

What can the scanner correct on a bad original?

THERE ARE MANY WAYS in which the scanner can correct a bad original. The main thing is that the designer should point out the fault to the color house and say what result is required. It helps the color house if the designer sends a sample to be matched when he or she returns the marked-up color proofs. In fact, it is best if a sample is supplied with the original, whether this is good or bad. If the color house is given a bad original with no instructions, it will assume that the task is to match the proof to the original.

The scanner can adjust exposure levels and contrast and remove color casts. However, any correction done on the scanner will affect the whole area of the original. Localized correction will involve either retouching by hand or the use of an electronic page make-up system, both of which can be expensive.

It is not really possible to correct a transparency which is too grainy. In this case the designer will need either to find a new original for the subject or to accept a result similar to the original.

Is it possible to improve detail?
To achieve what the designer wants here, the color house will increase shadows and weak middle tones to give a better range to the picture. A slight increase of yellow and black in blues/violets will neutralize the blue cast in the shadows. The increase in the shadows will probably be in the yellow, which will also make the browns in the rocks a richer color. This example shows how much improvement the color house can achieve.

BAD EXPOSURE

BAD CONTRAST

Can the contrast be improved?
To improve on this original, the color house will increase the highlights to give better modeling. Doing this will probably make the catchlights on the metal disappear to white, but this cannot be avoided.

Also, a reduction in the midtones will allow the colors to come through and "open out" the picture. The black highlight can also be reduced to brighten the picture. Again, a great improvement on the original.

Note that the color house will always try to match the transparency, unless asked to do otherwise, so if the designer wants a change or improvement, it must be requested before the color separation stage.

Can this image be made crisper?
To do this, the color house will increase the shadows, to give a better range. Also, it will increase the middle tones to give the mountain more contrast with the white building. Finally, it will probably increase the highlight contrast to give slightly more detail in the building.

Graininess sometimes needs to be retained as a design element, and here the designer should alert the color house to keep it.

IMAGE TOO SOFT

Can separation lose the color cast?

To lose the color cast here, the color house will reduce the cyan and magenta highlights and probably increase the yellow highlights.

The shadows will be made more neutral and the yellow increased in the midtone to make the brickwork warmer and more realistic. It could also be helpful to reduce the cyan midtones, allowing more of the warmth to come through.

There is a marked improvement here, showing what the scanner can achieve.

Can the scanner correct a damaged original?

IF THE ORIGINAL is scratched or torn, it can usually be repaired by hand–retouching (putting in dots by hand) or "pixelling" and copy brushing on an electronic page make-up system. Here, the system takes an area adjacent to the damage, measures the color content, and then reproduces it in the affected area.

Both methods can be expensive, and the designer should get a price before the color house starts work, as it may be cheaper to retouch the transparency and make a duplicate.

A Scitex operator (left) uses the "mouse" to retouch the required area. The area he is working on can be enlarged on the screen to give a greater degree of accuracy.

The torn original (above). Before asking the color house to retouch any damage, make sure you are quoted a price. Sometimes it may be cheaper to make a duplicate transparency and retouch that. Some electronic page make-up systems have the facility to output a repaired transparency.

Repairing a damaged image

1 The area to be worked on is shown on the screen. The operator has not only to repair the tear, but also to realign the two halves of the picture.

2 The system will take a pixel (see page 52) of the image from the green circle and duplicate it in the damaged area.

3 This shows the pixels being replaced. The green circle is as close to the tear as possible; this ensures that when the pixel is inserted in the tear, it matches those surrounding it.

4 This shows the tear taken out and the two halves of the picture realigned.

5 This is a 4,000 times enlargement showing the individual pixels.

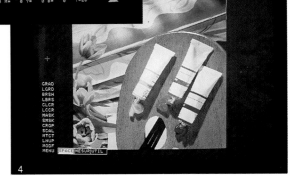

How much can an image be enlarged without loss of quality?

THE DESIGNER should be aware that different photographic films have different characteristics and some can bear enlargement better than others. Some 35mm films, for example, have a lot more grain than others, which may not show on the transparency but becomes much more apparent when enlarged.

As a general rule, it is best not to enlarge a 35mm transparency by more than 1000% (×10). Square 55mm transparencies do not have the same problems with grain as 35mm. However, they can hold a lot of detail that becomes apparent only on enlargement (such as hairs on a face).

Certain subjects, such as jewelry or food photography, can bear enlargement well. The reason is that these are normally shot in a studio under controlled lighting conditions.

If a subject has been enlarged too much, the only thing that can be done at the color proof stage to get a better quality image is to redesign the picture smaller and rescan it.

When the 5 × 4in (12.5 × 10cm) transparency (top) is enlarged, it is still sharp with well defined edges and no blurring.

When the 35mm (middle) is blown up to the same size it is un-sharp and shows the grain of the original transparency.

The 2¼ × 2¼in (5.7 × 5.7cm) (bottom) has no grain when blown up, but is still not as sharp as the 5 × 4in (12.5 × 10cm).

How should flat artwork be presented to the color house?

MOST SCANNERS have a drum around which the original is wrapped, so the flat artwork needs to be on a flexible board. If this is not possible, there are three ways of reproducing it. First, where artwork is painted on a rigid board, the color separation house can peel off the top surface to make it flexible. This can lead to creasing or other damage. In particular, poster paints are very brittle and when bent can crack and flake off.

Secondly, the rigid artwork can be reproduced with a graphic arts camera. The problem here is that the graphic arts camera (which preceded the scanner as a method of separation) is slow and expensive and lacks sophisticated electronic controls. Also, most color houses no longer have graphic arts cameras for color separation.

Where artwork cannot be flexible, it is probably best to make a color transparency from it and scan it in the normal way. This particularly applies when the original is valuable or is painted with poster paints.

Another reproduction problem with flat artwork occurs when strong solid colors (particularly fluorescent) are used by the artist. There are some colors that cannot be reproduced exactly by the four-color process. The designer can check this before reproduction by using a four-color tint chart to see how closely the color can be matched.

Flat artwork Try to avoid artwork that has to be peeled, because of the danger of damage. If an artwork is too valuable to risk damage, a transparency should be made, either 5 × 4 in (12.5 × 10 cm) or 10 × 8 in (25 × 20 cm). A transparency should also be made when the artwork is too big for the scanner. The transparency should include a gray scale and a color scale (right).

Marking up Give the color house as much information as possible. Inadequate instructions may make reproofing necessary, for which the client will have to pay. Mark up each overlay clearly and insert registration crosses on the base artwork and the overlays.

The finished proof (right) showing tints in position. A well marked-up piece of artwork has resulted in a good first proof.

overlay 1

overlay 2

base color artwork

register marks

base artwork

printer's instruction marked on each overlay as well

Base artwork print as 4 COL ½ tone
P.16 Ⓔ

Are some colors impossible to match using the four-color process?

NEITHER PHOTOGRAPHY nor color separation is a perfect process. The subject shot by the photographer has an infinite range of colors which is condensed on the transparency and further condensed in color separation. Four-color printing is therefore an approximation to the transparency, which itself is an approximation to the original subject. Both processes can get close but can never be perfect.

Normally, the process will come close enough to the original colors to be acceptable. However, serious problems can occur when a proprietary brand uses a special color that is difficult or impossible to match in the four-color process.

In general, the most difficult colors to reproduce are golds, deep blues, and certain greens. Some companies admit in their specifications that the corporate colors cannot be exactly matched out of the four process colors.

Pantone Process Color Simulator This shows special Pantone colors and their equivalents made up using tints of the four process colors. As you can see, the four-color process is unable to match the extra quality and range of color that the Pantone special color system offers.

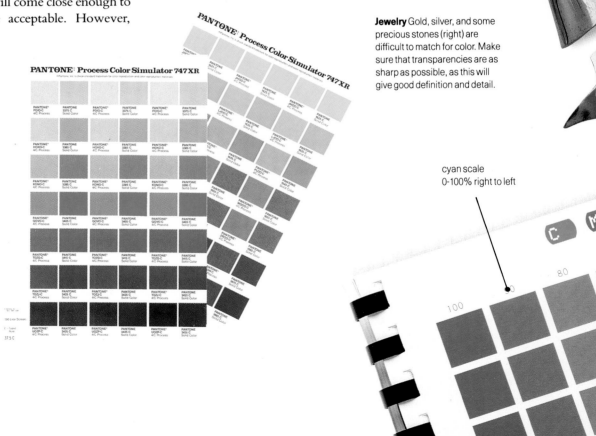

Jewelry Gold, silver, and some precious stones (right) are difficult to match for color. Make sure that transparencies are as sharp as possible, as this will give good definition and detail.

cyan scale
0-100% right to left

Packaging This sometimes requires special colors. An example is the Dunhill cigarette pack (left), printed in red and gold. The pack is printed in two colors – a special red and a special gold. If a transparency is made of the pack, it proves impossible to match the original red and gold, separating the transparency using the four process colors.

Using a tint chart will show you how close the four-color process can get to the special color. When comparing colors, remember to use an isolator (a black card with a square cut in it) so that the backgrounds do not give a false impression.

Tint charts (left) are often available free of charge from color houses, and every designer should have one. The layouts can vary but are usually self-explanatory. On this page, all the colors have 60% yellow and 0% black, with percentages of cyan and magenta ranging from 0% to 100%. Other pages show varying percentages of black and yellow.

yellow content
60% overall

C 0~100+ M 0~100+ Y

How to interpret this swatch: this represents
60% yellow
20% magenta
10% cyan
0% black

magenta scale
0-100% top to bottom

What are undercolour removal and achromatic reproduction?

ACHROMATIC

CONVENTIONAL

IN UNDERCOLOR REMOVAL the gray and neutral tones in the magenta, cyan, and yellow are removed and replaced with black. The main reason for doing this is that black ink is cheaper than the other three colors. Also, the less the weight of ink carried overall, the more control is possible on the press.

In conventional undercolor removal, most of the color and tone is still contributed by the three primary colors, with the black lending only deeper shadow tones. In achromatic reproduction, the very minimum amount of each color required is computed and the black added to produce the required depth of color. The process is intended to give no bias in the shadow areas, and using it will help to prevent "tracking" problems (see page 141), particularly when matching up two halves of a double-page spread. This is because the cyan, magenta, and yellow carry less ink and are therefore easier to control. Achromatic reproduction is still considered unproven, and the designer should not specify it unless it is proposed by the client or printer.

Overcoming tracking problems With ordinary separation and printing, any unexpected increase in the complementary color on press can affect the job. With achromatic separation the complementary colors are reduced so that this is unlikely to affect any hues of color. The example above shows the difference between a conventional and an achromatic print. Compare the two cyan separations – the achromatic set shows hardly any blue. Thus the joint of meat in the finished achromatic print has a truer color than that of the meat in the conventional tint example.

4-COLOR CONVENTIONAL

4-COLOR ACHROMATIC

UNDERCOLOR REMOVAL

CYAN + MAGENTA + YELLOW

BLACK

Conventional The three colors (cyan, magenta, and yellow) make up most of the picture, with black giving density and shape to the shadows and darker colors.

CYAN + MAGENTA + YELLOW

BLACK

Achromatic In achromatic reproduction the complementary colors are reduced as well as the shadows and middle tones, and replaced with a greatly increased black.

CYAN + MAGENTA + YELLOW

BLACK

Undercolor removal (UCR) UCR is used to subtract equal amounts of cyan, magenta, and yellow from shadows and dark degraded colors. These are then replaced by increased black.

What do I need to know about paper?

THERE IS AN INFINITE variety of papers, from the rather yellow, soggy newsprint used for newspapers to the brilliant white, glossy coated stock used for high-quality fashion magazines or art books.

But however good the color separation may be, the finished result can only be as good as the paper used. A color separation on newsprint will have dull highlights because the areas that should be white are off-white or gray. Also, the dots used in the separation process sink into the absorbent material and spread. By contrast, on a glossy white paper, the highlights are bright and the dots lie on the surface and are sharp, giving a crisp, clean result.

Probably the most commonly used paper in publishing and advertising is matte-coated. This is white and has a surface that is coated to appear matte rather than glossy. The advantage of this is that the surface is smooth enough to give good, sharp reproduction of color, without the problem of legibility of a gloss paper, which produces reflections that can be an obstacle to reading.

The color house needs to know the type of paper being used, as the screen rulings and dot gains will be different for different papers. In addition, the color house should proof on the same type of paper that will be used for the final printed job. If this is not specified, the job might well be proofed on a glossy paper and printed on an uncoated paper. The printed result would be nowhere near as good as the proof, and the client could complain or reject the job, even though uncoated paper was specified in the first place.

Within each type of paper (e.g. coated, book, text, cover, offset) there are scores of different makes. It can be costly or inconvenient to obtain the actual make of paper to proof on, and although this is the ideal, it is normally sufficient to use the correct type of paper rather than the identical brand on which the job will be printed.

Paper is made in different weights, and the proofs should be on the same weight as the final job.

A point to bear in mind is that different papers have different drying times, so some jobs cannot be pushed through quickly at printing stage.

Coated paper used with a fine screen This book is printed on a matte art coated paper, which takes a fairly fine screen (in this case 150), as the ink lies on the surface of the paper, rather than being absorbed and thus spreading, which would give too large a dot.

Showthrough With some lighter papers, lack of opacity can result in "showthrough," which is when the image on the other side of the paper shows through as a dark shadow. It is particularly noticeable (below) when the side you are looking at is mainly white paper and the reverse side is printed with a large, dark area.

Newsprint used with a fine screen Newsprint is very absorbent, and when too fine a screen is used (here it is 150) the ink bleeds into the paper and the dots join together. You can see this clearly in the enlargement.

Newsprint used with a coarse screen Here newsprint is shown with a coarser screen (85) which is much more suitable for this paper. A 65 or 85 screen used on newsprint gives enough room between each dot for the ink to bleed into the paper without the dots joining up. However, the coarser screen makes it difficult to get a good density of color.

How does screen size affect proofing?

Conventional dot shapes
Conventional contact screens are still widely used for mono halftone work. More subtle changes in tonal value are produced by elliptical dot screens, compared to square dot screens.

Scanner dot shapes Scanners can produce a range of dot shapes as required, the commonest being square. Dots can be round or elliptical. There is no great difference in quality, though square dots are said to give a better definition if the image being reproduced is, for example, a computer screen.

THE SIZE OF THE DOT in color separation is governed by the screen ruling. Before scanners were developed, color separation was carried out using a glass or film screen ruled to make a grid. The light was transmitted through the spaces between the grid lines to create dots of the required size. The screen ruling is therefore the number of lines per inch.

The standard screen rulings are (in lines per inch) 65, 85, 100, 120, 133, 150, 200, and 300.

The choice of screen ruling depends mainly on the type of paper being used: the rougher the paper, the coarser the screen required. Newspapers printed on newsprint might use 85 screen, on uncoated offset paper 120 or 133 screen, and on matte-coated paper 150 screen.

Most publication or advertising color work is printed on matte- or gloss-coated paper and is therefore 150 screen. If you do not specify a screen ruling, the color house will normally work to 150. The screen ruling will be specified in the printer's specification sheet (see page 32).

Although 150 is the finest screen used in normal commercial printing, some printers specialize in the high-quality printing of black and white or color halftones for photographic books, medical textbooks, or photographs of coins. Here, screens as fine as 200 or even 300 are used. To reproduce these properly, a very smooth expensive paper is needed.

65 LINES PER INCH

85 LINES PER INCH

100 LINES PER INCH

Standard screens On newsprint the standard screen is 85; most magazines are 133 or 150; high-quality work on good paper can be up to as much as 300. If the separation has been done abroad, check whether a metric screen ruling has been used.

120 LINES PER INCH

150 LINES PER INCH

133 LINES PER INCH

200 LINES PER INCH

ENLARGED DETAIL SHOWING HALFTONE DOT

Special screens Some screens can be used in the design of the job. You can use mezzo or square line or cut-line screens. Check with your color house to see if it has these. In the spread (above) two different screen dots have been used to create a textured feel. On the left-hand page, the image was screened at 125, while the image on the right-hand page was screened at 25.

What are scanner effects?

M<small>OST</small> <small>SCANNERS</small> can achieve picture distortion, and most electronic page make-up systems can carry out pixellations, vignetting, and copy brushing.

When requesting special effects, bear in mind that they can be quite expensive, and ask the color house to quote a price before starting work.

Distortion These two examples of distortion (right and far right) show just what can be achieved using this scanning technique. The female model has been squeezed by about 50%; the chrome headlight has been stretched by 150%.

Ghosting The technique used here (right) involved reproducing an image at a reduced strength of dot, in this case 20%.

Pixellation The word "pixel" comes from PICture ELements, which are the minute image areas created by digitizing a picture. Pixellation means reducing the number of pixels in an image, then enlarging them to give an overall effect. The image of the bird (right) has been pixellated, and the group picture (far right) mixes pixellation with montage techniques.

A GREAT WALL EVERY TIME.

Polycell
All Purpose
Wallpaper
Adhesive
NOW WITH PVA!

Montaging In the image (above) an illustration and a transparency have been montaged. The wallpaper is real, as is the tree, but the landscape, which includes the Great Wall, is all illustration.

Trick effects The dynamic image (below) shows the full and unique potential of scanner effects used creatively.

PUZZLE

The Human Adventure is Just Beginning

How are final films produced?

Where the color house does not have an electronic page make-up system, the following methods are used to arrive at final film. First the line artwork (CRC) is shot. This film is then given to the scanner operator, who will size the transparency. The transparency is then mounted and scanned.

The job is then passed to a planner, who will "opaque" the line negative. This is then taped down onto a sheet of clear plastic foil which has been punched to ensure register with the foils for the other three colors. The planner then plans the negatives of all the color halftones in one of the four colors. The next stage is to cut masks on a fifth foil to crop the halftones exactly as required and cut masks for any areas of tint appearing. The required tints are then taped to another foil.

The foils are then contacted in a light frame to positive film, using the mask for the halftones laid on top of the halftones for one exposure. The planner next contacts the foil with the foil of tints

Sizing transparencies It is crucial that the transparency is sized correctly, otherwise it will have to be rescanned. Here, the scanner operator is measuring the distance between two points on the layout.

The operator then measures exactly the same points on the transparency. For this, it is important that the original trace be clearly drawn.

Dividing the required size on the layout by the size on the original gives the percentage enlargement (100% = same size).

Sizing color transparency

Shooting line artwork

Shooting line The original line artwork (including any type) is shot to the required size on a graphic arts camera.

Spotting out line The line negative is spotted out with opaque to eliminate any paste-up marks or dust spots.

Proofing by Matchprint, Cromalin or to make plates for wet proofing

Preparing masks for tints and halftones

Preparing final four-color positive film

Preparing foil and positioning negative halftone

Four-color scanning

Spotting and retouching film

Scanning The transparency is scanned, taking into account the printer's specifications and any comments from the customer. The scanner will produce either negatives or positives – usually negatives.

and the appropriate mask and makes a second exposure onto the film. Finally, another mask for register and trim marks is exposed onto the film. At this stage the final film of one of the four colors has been completed.

This final positive film is used as a guide, and the other three colors are planned to fit with this and then contacted to the final positive as above, with black type being exposed onto the film for the black. The final films then go for proofing.

ELECTRONIC PAGE MAKE-UP SYSTEMS

More and more color houses are using electronic page make-up systems. A typical piece of final film (top) produced by such a system shows all the elements in position. With electronic page make-up systems, color transparencies are scanned in the traditional way on a drum scanner. The next stage is to feed the images into the system, then the operator manipulates and combines type, tint panels and pictures on screen, following the designer's layout (above).

Color proofs that have been generated electronically can be corrected conventionally – since going back to the electronic system can be too expensive.

What are the different types of proofs?

THERE ARE NOW several types of color proof available, but they can be divided into two types – wet proofs made on a proofing press and off-machine proofs.

WET PROOFS (also described as machine proofs) are achieved by making an aluminum printing plate from the separated film and printing it on a flat-bed proofing press, using the ink and paper that will be used on the final printed job.

The proofing press is actually a printing machine which is much slower than the press on which the job will finally be printed. The sheets of paper are fed by hand, and the machine prints only one or two colors at a time rather than all four. It is not possible to produce more than a few dozen four-color sheets an hour, compared with six or seven thousand on a printing press.

The advantage of wet proofing is that the designer can see something that is virtually identical to the final result and on the correct paper. Also, it has cost advantages where several proofs are required, as a proofing press can produce up to 24 sets of proofs economically, which is not possible with off-machine proofs.

The disadvantage is that it is more expensive and time-consuming when only one or two proofs are required, which is often the case. This is because a plate has to be made, and this cannot be re-used for the actual printing if any corrections are necessary.

OFF-MACHINE PROOFS have been developed within the last ten years and use photographic rather than printing techniques. The two most common systems are Cromalin, manufactured by Du Pont, and Matchprint, from 3M. In the Cromalin system, a sheet of white board is laminated with an ultra-violet light-sensitive laminate, the film is exposed onto it, and the exposed image is then colored with toner. The operation is repeated to achieve all four colors. A color bar is included in the proof in order to check density, dot gain, and gray balance.

In the Matchprint system, instead of using toner for the colors, a color film is laminated to a sheet of white board, the film is exposed to it and then it is processed to give the first color. This is repeated until all four colors have been built up on the board. Again a color bar is incorporated.

COLOR KEY is an earlier 3M system still in use, in which four separate sheets of color film are placed

Scatter proofs Also described as random proofs, this method of proofing is often used for books or simple magazines. They are cheaper than page proofs, as they do not include type matter and so the pictures fit on far fewer sheets.

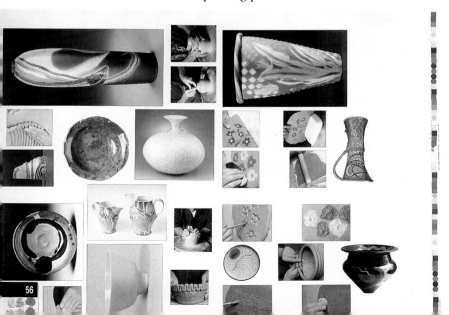

on top of each other and mounted on white paper. The color achieved on this system is less accurate than that produced by Cromalin or Matchprint.

SCATTER PROOFS To produce these the color house scans the originals, masks them to size and imposes them to fit as many as possible on a proof sheet. Scatter proofs do not include type matter and are not laid out in the correct position relative to each other.

Scatter proofs can be the correct solution in two situations. First, where price is paramount and the job has only two or three pictures per page and a fairly staple layout. Here the color can be approved and the color house can send final film to the printer to do the page make-up, rather than have it done by the color house. The designer would still see an imposed blueprint from the color house to check positioning of pictures relative to type.

Scatter proofs are also used for a more complex job as a check on the color quality before the color house does make-up. This is more expensive, as it involves two stages of proofing, but the cost can be justified when quality is paramount.

PAGE PROOFS show the type in position and include all tint panels, etc., exactly as they will appear in the final job. They can be supplied as pairs of pages (double-page spreads) or imposed to the printer's imposition.

The advantage of imposed proofs is that the tracking (see page 141) can be checked, so that if one subject needs to carry a lot of magenta ink, for example, the designer can see what effect this will have on other subjects in the same track and make the necessary adjustments before the printing stage.

The growth in popularity of electronic page make-up systems has made the use of page proofs much more common than previously.

All systems mentioned above are economical where only one or two proofs are required, but there is a

problem in that the proofs have a higher dot gain than wet proofs or printing. This means that colors are more intense and the designer has to make allowance for this when checking color.

FUTURE DEVELOPMENTS IN PROOFING include direct digital color proofing (DDCP), in which the proofing system is linked directly to the scanner or page make-up system. The system takes the stored digital information, records it on an optical disk, and outputs it through a digital writer onto the job paper, using liquid colors. The system is computer controlled, giving control of density, dot gain, and other characteristics. The proof is identical to the finished printed result.

REMOTE MONITORS will become a common method of proofing in the future, particularly in high-volume magazine and advertising work. Here, the design studio will have a color visual display unit linked to the color house, and this display can be checked both for color and layout. Because the color is not yet very accurate, this would be a "first proof," with the designer probably seeing a conventional form of proof before printing.

Thermal prints These are similar to DTP-produced laser proofs but in four color. In terms of color quality, they are no match for a proper proof. However, they offer a good visual reference to what the final printed piece will look like and are useful for checking the position of elements before the color house pushes the button for the color proof run.

What are progressives?

WHEN MAKING WET PROOFS, the color house will automatically make a set of progressive proofs at the same time as producing the four-color proofs. Progressives show how the four-color result is built up, one color at a time. A set of progressives would therefore consist of seven sheets. Each sheet is shown on this spread, though the sequence in which they are built up can vary from one color house or printer to another.

Before four-color printing presses were common, color was printed one or two colors at a time and progressives were essential for the printer, to avoid putting too much or too little color on the first three colors and becoming aware of it only when the last color was printed. With the use of four-color presses, progressives are less necessary.

When a designer is checking proofs, it can be helpful to also have the progressives, but only if the designer has the depth of technical knowledge to be able to make use of them. This very often involves also checking them with a densitometer (see page 75). In practice, however, most designers and clients do not check progressives, but on approval of proofs they are sent with the film to the printer.

It is not economical to make progressives using off-machine proofing methods such as Cromalin or Matchprint.

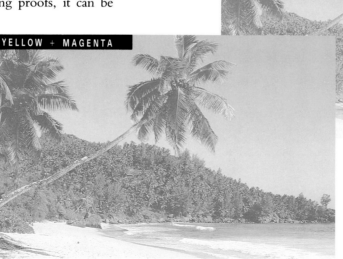

YELLOW + MAGENTA + CYAN

MAGENTA

YELLOW + MAGENTA

YELLOW

4-COLOR

CYAN

BLACK

CYAN

Progressive proofs These show how the final color is built up. The films were proofed up in the correct printing sequence. The yellow is printed first, then the magenta, then the cyan, giving a three-color process, and finally the black.

HOW DO I CHECK A PROGRESSIVE?

A great deal can be checked on progressives. At this stage it is best to use a densitometer to check ink weights and dot gains. The color house will read the densities and dot gains. You can also check the screen angles, and with some experience it is possible to tell a lot about each color, check whether any shadows have filled in, and check that the highlights are printing in all colors, so as not to give any bias. You will need a linen tester to do this checking. Also check the actual color of ink, as sometimes the proofs are not washed properly, resulting in inks dirtying the image.

Ultimately, the best check an inexperienced designer can make is to look at the four-color proof only – progessives can be confusing to the untrained eye.

A variety of instruments are available for checking proofs; here a specialist densitometer is being used to ensure the film dot size is correct.

How does the color separation house correct color?

IF THE DESIGNER considers the color proof not to be a good match to the original, the color separation house can effect corrections as follows:

RESCANNING Here the color house repeats the whole scanning procedure, but takes into account the corrections on the proof. The scanner can be adjusted to make any or all of the four colors stronger or weaker, improve definition and brightness, and improve highlights or detail and many other characteristics. However, all these corrections must be done to the whole of the subject, as the scanner cannot deal with a specific area. Rescanning is the most common way of correcting color.

MASKING Localized correction of the subject (for example, to make a face less red without reducing the red elsewhere in the picture) is done by masking off the area to be corrected and then contacting that area from negative to positive, varying exposure

CORRECTION COSTS

If a correction is required because of unsatisfactory work by the color house, there will be no charge. However, the color house will obviously charge for any corrections that represent a change of mind by the designer or client. These corrections can be expensive and thus lead to possible conflict between designer and client or designer and color house.

The safest course is to make sure that the client is shown detailed layouts or finished roughs and told of the financial penalties and possible time delay of changes of mind at proof stage.

On a scale of 1 to 10

Rescanning
10
Recropping bigger
8
Recropping smaller
7
Changing tint
4
Imposing a tint
4
Deletion
1
Moving type
1-5

Line work To delete type (above), you mask it out on the black negative and make a new, black final positive. To strip in new type, you must have it shot, stripped into the black negative and contacted to a new final positive.

To reposition a bullet, which affects four colors, means remasking on the negatives for all four films and contacting four new final films.

Masking The vase (below) would need to be dry-dot etched to reduce all the colors. The retoucher makes a mask for the area of the vase and then contacts the colors to negative – with an increased exposure on the required area – before contacting them back to final positives.

time to increase or decrease the size of the dot in the area to be altered. Increasing the dot size strengthens the color, and decreasing it weakens the color. This technique is known as dry-dot etching.

HAND RETOUCHING is more expensive than the above two methods, and most color separation houses employ far fewer retouchers than were used in the past, because the improvements in scanners have resulted in less need for retouching.

Retouching is done using chemicals. The retoucher applies a staging lacquer to areas that are to remain unchanged, then applies chemicals to the film to reduce the size of the dots on the positive. If the dots have to be *increased* in size, then the retoucher works on a negative.

ELECTRONIC RETOUCHING On electronic page make-up systems, it is possible, though expensive, to correct the color of the smallest area very accurately. This is because the system is capable of removing the dots of a color in a particular area and replacing them with dots of any size. Taken to the extreme, the system can actually change the color of a subject to a completely different color. The high hourly cost rate of such systems means that they cannot economically be used for corrections that can easily be carried out by the above methods. Also, if the correction required is an author's correction, it may be worth getting a price before proceeding. The term "author's correction" is used to describe any correction for which the color separation house can make an extra charge. It may be a change requested by the client, the copywriter, or the designer.

1

2

3

4

Electronic retouching To improve the contrast and detail in a specific area, it is best to retouch it on a system (below). First make a mask for the area required and then reduce the highlights and increase the shadows.

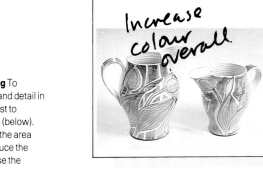

Rescan To increase color and contrast overall on the vases, it is best to rescan (above).

Hand retouching To reduce the magenta on the vase (above), the retoucher first applies an enamel paint to the positive to protect the dots in the background of the picture. The exposed area is then treated with chemicals, making the dots smaller on the vase only.

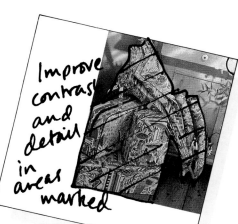

To increase the dot The illustration above demonstrates diagrammatically the method used to increase the dot size when correcting color.
1 Original film showing dot to be corrected. **2** The retoucher goes back to the negative film and masks off the (red) dots not to be worked on. **3** The unmasked dot is treated and made larger. **4** A new positive is made with the resulting larger dot.

To reduce the dot the retoucher would simply work on the positive, masking the dots to be left alone, and etching back the dot concerned.

What is dot gain?

THIS TERM describes the increase in the size of the dot caused by the processes that the image goes through between film and printing. The dot can grow at the following stages: platemaking (the exposed dot on the plate is bigger than the film dot); ink (tends to spread slightly beyond the dot area); printing on the blanket; blanket printing on the paper.

Other factors that affect the amount of dot gain include cylinder pressure, type of printing plate, and type of printing machine (particularly if web- or sheet-fed, as web produces much more dot gain). The type of paper is also an important factor.

Dot gain is measured as the percentage by which the proofed or printed dot is larger than the original film dot. A wet proof has a dot gain of around 12% and off-machine proofs (for example, Cromalin) around 24%.

It would clearly be unacceptable for printed jobs to have stronger colors than originals or proofs, so the color separation house has to ensure that the dot on the film is made artificially smaller than it should be. In this way the finished result is faithful to the original, despite dot gain.

Cross-section through paper showing ink absorption Dot gain is a combination of mechanical gain (depending on ink, type of paper, plates, and press, which all influence the degree to which the ink sinks into the paper) and optical dot gain whereby the halftone dot on top of the paper gives a colored shadow on the paper.

Dot gain tolerances The images (opposite) show various tolerances from the norm, in this case for the magenta film. These tolerances vary depending on cylinder pressure, age of rollers, temperature, and so on. and demonstrate the variations which are acceptable in the mid-tones – that is, in the 50% dot. Obviously with highlight dots – which are normally about 3% – the tolerances are less, and the tolerances in the shadow area are less critical. Your separation house will have the spec sheet that tells them the dot gain factor of your printing and will adjust the dot to that dot gain, working within those tolerances.

+ 2% MAGENTA

− 2% MAGENTA

REFERENCE STANDARD

+ 4% MAGENTA

− 4% MAGENTA

The effect of paper on dot gain
As these enlargements show, an image reproduced on good-quality paper (top) shows the correct dot gain, giving sharp dots. When it is reproduced on newsprint (above) the dots bleed into the paper.

What is moiré?

When a subject is printed, the dots of each color are at a certain angle (see pages 72-73). If the dots of one color are at the wrong angle, they will clash with the others, thus causing a moiré pattern. This happens most commonly on tints that are laid manually. It can also occur when two tints overlap.

Moiré patterning in four-color sets is caused by something in the original interfering with the pattern of dots in the set. This often happens when a previously printed copy is scanned, and in this case the pattern of dots on the original clashes with the new pattern of dots on the scanned set.

Other subjects that can give rise to moiré include fabrics of fine houndstooth and Prince of Wales checks; tiling on roofs; photographs of pictures on TV screens; stereo loudspeakers. The color separation house can alleviate the problem by reducing the detail, but this can affect the overall picture.

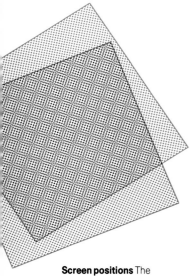

Screen positions The enlargement (above) shows the moiré effect caused when screens are positioned at the wrong angles. The two tints on the right will not clash when they are laid exactly on top of each other, at the correct angles.

Shoot dot for dot The moiré effect (right) is caused by having rescanned a previously printed image. The screen of the original separation is clashing with the screen of the new separation.

One solution (below) is to shoot the previously printed image dot for dot (on a camera not a scanner). This can only be done if the new separation is a similar size to the original. Otherwise the screen will be too coarse if enlarged and if reduced, too fine.

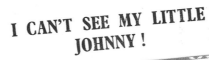

I CAN'T SEE MY LITTLE JOHNNY !

Soften dot Another solution is to put the original slightly out of focus, which makes the dots in the background merge into each other (above). However, this can result in some loss of detail.

Different sizes (right) and different screen rulings will have varying effects on moiré. In general, the larger the image, the less chance there is of moiré occurring.

Duotones This duotone (left) on a tint background has several overlapping tints; this increases the risk of moiré, as more screen angles are involved.

What are the industry standards and specifications?

Swop is the organization of Specifications Web Offset Publications, which has issued specifications for American offset publications. The specifications have been arrived at after discussion with agencies, separators, publishers, and printers, and in most of the U.S. are widely accepted. They are used for gravure publication proofing as well.

The need for some form of specification arises from the fact that separations for magazines can come from many sources, and that in order to get good results on high-speed presses the separators of the film need to work toward a common standard.

The SWOP specifications apply to prepress process factors such as proofing paper, type, and proofing characteristics such as dot gain, density, and gray balance. If applied correctly adherence to these specifications means that an advertisement appearing in many magazines will be consistently reproduced by different printers and in different magazines.

COLOR BARS The most common control bars are shown here.

INK for web offset publication proofs are encompassed by SWOP, which has made recommendations to separation houses. These recommendations advise that SWOP proofing inks be used to ensure that magenta, cyan, and process yellow inks be comparable in color at all houses, even if the process inks are made by different manufacturers. An exact match of proof and production ink is not easily achieved due to environmental and application constraints. Printers have, however, come close to using the same color, and the same consistency of color, for production inks as are found in proofing inks. Other countries' four-color process inks differ slightly from SWOP. Japanese inks, which are also used in Hong Kong, in particular have stronger, brighter colors. In practice, most jobs can be proofed using SWOP inks and printed abroad using local standard inks without major problems. However, where quality is critical, the designer should ensure that the separation house obtains ink from the foreign printer for proofing.

THE PANTONE SYSTEM

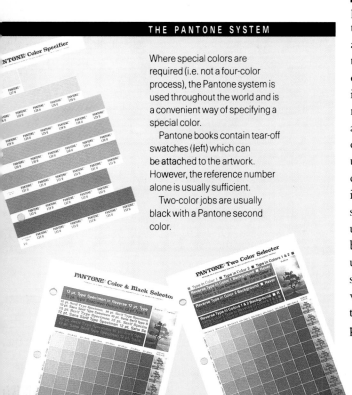

Where special colors are required (i.e. not a four-color process), the Pantone system is used throughout the world and is a convenient way of specifying a special color.

Pantone books contain tear-off swatches (left) which can be attached to the artwork. However, the reference number alone is usually sufficient.

Two-color jobs are usually black with a Pantone second color.

Color bars There are various makes of color bar. However, although they look different, they all share common elements (see page 70-71 for details). These are all for four-color sheet-fed offset, but there are special color bars available for 6-color work and web-offset printing.
Top to bottom:
Dupont Brunner Cromalin

GCA/GATF Proof Comparator II. The separation house makes a reference proof from the Proof Comparator films and sends it to the designer for subsequent referral. Thereafter all proofs that the color house sends to the agency are accompanied by an image of the Proof Comparator. The designer then compares his or her reference image with the one on the proof.
GCA/GATF 85 line inch Color Bar (used for newsprint, hence the coarser screen)
Gretag Matchprint
Gretag Wet Proof
Kinmei Printing Color Bar (Japanese Printing Company).

At first glance these color bars may all look very different. However, each bar contains the same basic elements.
1 Percentage screen patches.
2 Solid patches.
3 Coarse and fine screen patches.
4 Trapping patches.
5 Gray balance patch.
6 Highlight dot and microline patches.

The color bars on this spread should not be used for any form of checking. They are reproduced here as examples for discussion only.

MAGENTA | BLACK
YELLOW | CYAN

Eurostandard CROMALIN*

DU PONT
CROMALIN® DuZ ...it's a registered trademark

© 1979 Felix Brunner CH-6611 Corippo

Soltanto le strisce originali di controllo
Eurostandard CROMALIN®/system Brunner
con il numero di fabbricazione gofrato
devono essere utilizzate.
L'impiego di altre copiatrici limitate/retypes,
o falsificati sarà perseguito legalmente.

C+M+Y B C+Y C C+M M M+Y Y 3×80% 3×50%

50% B   50% C, 41% M, 41% Y

GCA/GATF Proof Comparator II©

YMCK

P

MATCHPRINT® COLOR ELEMENT 3M

Made by GRETAG

WHITE 20% 40% 60% 80% CYAN C+M 20% 40% 60% 80% MAGENTA M+Y 20% 40% 60% 80% YELLOW C+Y 20% 40% 60% 80% BLACK C+M+Y

LASER DOTS   BALANCE   NORMAL DOTS

SLUR

C M B Y

BL C M Y

HOW TO CHECK

COLOR PROOFS

2

This section explains in detail what the designer should look for when checking proofs; the equipment required to do the job properly; how to mark up proofs; and what color bars are used for.

Examples are shown of proofs that are up or down in each of the four process colors or incorrect in other ways. Different subjects can present very different reproduction problems, and examples of food, fashion, furniture, jewelry, and other subjects are given, showing what can go wrong and how to correct it.

The section concludes with some color house "nightmares."

How can color bars help the designer check proofs?

On pages 66-67, you can see a range of international color bars. Although they look different, they all measure the same characteristics, and once you have learned how to read one color bar, you should be able to read all of them.

On this spread we look in detail at a Brunner color bar.
1 25% and 75% screen patches.
2 Solid patches.
3 Coarse and fine screen patches.
4 Trapping patches.
5 Gray balance patch.
6 Highlight dot and microline patches.

The color bar on this spread should not be used for any form of checking. It is reproduced here as an example for discussion only.

WHEN FILM is prepared for proofing, a film of the color bar (original, not duplicate film) is put on the edge of each piece of film. The color bar then appears on the edge of the proof and can be checked for the characteristics shown here. The main point of using a color bar is to check that the proof (and subsequently the printing) is carrying the correct weight of ink and that the plate (either the proofing plate or the printing plate) has been correctly exposed. If not, then it is difficult to check the color proof properly, since if the proofing process has applied too much or too little of a particular color, the designer will find it difficult to check the separation. A color bar is also essential for comparing dot gain (see pages 62-63).

Similarly, at the printing stage the printer will compare his color bar with the one on the proof, and if they are identical the printed result should be identical to the proof. If not, it means that the film of the subject is different from the proof, possibly due

C+M+Y   C+Y   C   C+M   M   M+Y

Trapping patches (left) Trapping happens when the first color dries too much, which prevents the following colors from being absorbed into the paper. It gives a mottled effect, but can be measured only on a programmed densitometer.

Druckkontrollstreifen © 1981 system Brunner

1   1   2   3   3   2   3   3   2   4   4   2   4   2   4   2   1   1   2   3   3   5   6

0,5%	1%	6µ 8µ		0,5%	1%	6µ 8µ		0,5%	1%	6µ 8µ		0,5%	1%	6µ 8µ		0,5%	1%	6µ 8µ
2%	3%	11		2%	3%	11		2%	3%	11		2%	3%	11		2%	3%	11
4%	5%	13 16		4%	5%	13 16		4%	5%	13 16		4%	5%	13 16		4%	5%	13 16

Plate under exposed | Accepted Production Tolerance | Plate exposed to meet recommendation | Accepted Production Tolerance | Plate over exposed

Positive plate exposure (left) These enable the printer and proofer to check that the plates have been exposed correctly. On an underexposed plate the dots are too heavy and on an overexposed plate they start to disappear.

to correction after proof stage.

As with progressives (see pages 58–59), the reading of color bars is something most designers are not trained to do. Some therefore prefer to regard them as a tool for the color separation house and printer. However, if you experiment with reading color bars, you can gain a useful understanding of their value.

Designers who know how to use a densitometer, check the color bar to see if the proofing is correct. First, read the solid areas of each color for the ink densities (see below) and then read the specified tint areas to check the dot gain. If one of the colors has been proofed with either the wrong dot gain or density, it will affect the neutral gray areas on the color bar, and this will help you to identify which color is incorrect. Gray balance is 50% dot on cyan and 38% to 40% on magenta and yellow.

Manufacturers of densitometers use slightly different filters in the instrument's reading head, and the readings can differ according to whether narrow- or broad-band filters are used. The designer should check the comparison chart that is normally supplied by the manufacturer.

DENSITY is the light-stopping or light-absorbing ability of an object and is measured in printing on a logarithmic scale ranging from 0.0 to 3.0. It is measured with a densitometer.

Printers set up their presses to their own standards, which are set out in the printer's specification (see page 32). Smaller presses have smaller inking rollers, which exert less pressure and are therefore not capable of carrying the same weight of ink as bigger presses. With a small press the printer will use slightly lower ink densities.

Checking plate exposure
(below) A visual guide for the platemaker for checking plate exposure. If the crosses within the circles disappear then there is something wrong with the plate exposure.

50%   50%

Dot gain (right) The coarse screen 50% gives you an at-a-glance check on dot gain. The fine screen can be read with a densitometer programmed with the Murray Davies equation, which gives the exact amount of dot gain. These are shown (left) enlarged.

Super

Barre de contrôle de l'impression © 1981 system Brunner CH-6600 Locarno

Print Control Strip © 1981 system Brunner CH-6600 Locarno

Balance (left) This enables you to see immediately whether all the colors are proofed in balance. When proofed correctly, it should appear as a neutral gray.

Balance

Density (left) The individual solid colors (cyan, magenta, yellow, and black) are for reading the ink densities, which should match the printer's specifications.

B   C   M   Y

How do I check screen ruling and angles?

DIFFERENT COLORS have different screen angles, and if the angles are not correct, moire patterning can result (see pages 64–65). Normally, the color separation house has the scanner set up properly, so the designer need not check the screen angles on every proof, but only if there is a problem such as moiré.

Screen testers To check the screen angles, keep the bottom edge of the tester square to the bottom of the picture, and a circle will appear around a line on the tester. For example, on the magenta it will appear around 45%. To check the screen ruling, lay the tester on the film and turn it until a star shape appears with one corner pointing to the screen number. Your repro house will supply you with both testers as they are part of its standard equipment.

4-COLOR

2-COLOR

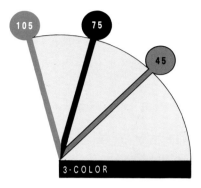

3-COLOR

Halftone screens These are placed at an angle of 45° (opposite page, top right) so that the pattern of dots produced is not visible to the eye. Compare with the 90° screen (opposite page, top left).

Checking angles It is important to make sure that all colors are at the correct angles, otherwise moiré patterning can occur. In four-color printing (above) the magenta is at 45°; the cyan is 105° (this can also be called 15° – they are the same); the black is 75°; the yellow is 90°.

Checking two-color angles The lightest color is on the most prominent angle – 75°, and the black on 45°.

Checking three-color angles This is the same as two-color, but the third color is angled at 105° (15°).

Using a tester The angle tester is kept square to the picture, and the circle appears around the 75° line. It is always best to measure the angle on a 50% tone, otherwise the highlights are too light and the shadows too dark to read properly. Here the angle tester is being used on film, but it can also be used on color proofs, though the angles are less easy to see.

What equipment do I need to check proofs?

To check proofs properly, you will need certain equipment. The items described below make the job easier and the designer more efficient.

TRANSPARENCY VIEWER (lightbox) These are available in various sizes, but what is more important is that the lighting conform to the national standard of PH2.30-1989. This standard defines the color and intensity of the light source and is the one to which most transparency viewers used at color separation houses and printers conform. This means that the transparency is viewed under the same lighting conditions at the various stages of reproduction and printing. Make sure that the tubes are replaced at the recommended intervals.

VIEWING BOOTH Although bulkier than transparency viewers, viewing booths can be obtained in sizes as small as 11½ × 16½, small enough to fit into the most crowded studio. They are used to view the proofs and flat artwork. The lighting in the viewing booth should conform to the national standard of PH2.30-1989.

SCREEN-ANGLE TESTER The different process colors have different screen angles (see pages 72-73), and the tester consists of a piece of film. Your color separation house will probably be able to let you have one free of charge.

SCREEN TESTER This tests the screen ruling. Like the screen-angle tester, it consists of a piece of film

and should be obtainable from your color house.

LINEN TESTER This is the type of magnifying glass used by color separation houses and printers to view 35mm color transparencies. The folding stand means that the lens is the correct distance from the subject and the hands are left free. The linen tester is used to view both transparencies and color proofs.

A **35mm transparency** (below) is difficult to view and needs to be magnified to check detail areas. The naked eye is usually sufficient to check color proofs, and magnification with a linen tester is usually needed only to check register or damaged film

Most designers have transparency viewers, but very few have viewing booths (left) despite the fact that they are essential for proper color correction. Without a viewing booth, the colors of the proof will be affected by both the type of lighting in use in the studio and outside weather conditions. This makes it very difficult to correct color accurately.

DO I NEED A DENSITOMETER?

A densitometer (right) is a sophisticated and expensive electronic device used to check the density of ink on a proof by reading the color bars (see pages 66-67). It cannot be used without a deeper technical knowledge than is required of most designers, and is not essential.

Color separation houses and printers use it to compare the densities of proofs, film, color bars, and the final printed result.

What are the basic elements to check?

Backgrounds of tints or special colors If a common special color or tint background is required for several pages in a publication, the designer should be aware of problems the printer might have in maintaining consistency between pages.

For example, if a buff background is used, consisting of a percentage tint of process yellow, and there are some pages that require a heavy weight of yellow to be run for the pictures, the tints on those pages will be heavier than on the other pages. The use of a special fifth color (a Pantone color, for example) for the backgrounds only should prevent this problem. But remember that it is more expensive to run five colors than four.

Color bar This tells the designer whether the proof is faithful to the film being proofed. For example, if the proofer has used too much yellow ink, so that the proof looks too yellow even though the film is correct, the color bar will show this.

WHAT IS REJECTABLE?

If a proof is bad either because the color is way out, or because the layout, sizing, or position has been done incorrectly, there may be a case for rejecting it without the client or designer checking it, on the grounds that the client would be so disappointed that he would lose confidence in the designer or color house. However, even though a proof may not be shown to the client, it is usually worthwhile for the designer to check it, as there may be a design error as well as the color house's mistake, and changing it at this stage saves a further proof later.

Rejection can also occur when the client and designer insist on a reproof because the checked proof is so different from the original that the designer, without seeing a reproof, cannot be confident that correction will be carried out properly.

B·I·R·T·H·D·A·Y G·I·F·T·S

With the help of a supply of homemade sweets there is no need to ever despair of what to give someone for a present. Nearly everyone has a hobby or interest that can provide the spark of inspiration to turn a 'useful' everyday item into something rather special – homemade sweets show that care and thought have gone into the present.

·SUGAR MICE·
Instructions for making sugar mice are given on page 157, but as many people are animal lovers adapt the instructions to make an appropriate type of animal such as a pet dog or cat. Tie a ribbon and bow around its neck. ▼

·TANKARD·
Beer drinkers are not the only people who would appreciate a glass mug or tankard – 300 ml (½ pint) sizes are useful for fruit juices or other soft drinks, such as, Bucks Fizz (sparkling wine and orange juice), Black velvet (Guinness and sparkling wine) or Pimms. ▼

·LOLLIPOPS·
Choose three or four flavourings and appropriate colourings of lollipops as an alternative to sweets. Kids will love to find their favourite lollies in a bright new pair of wellies. ▶

·TRAIN·
When buying toys for children, choose ones that can be filled with sweets. Add a shipment of edible freight ▲ to the ever-popular toy train set.

·NUMBERS·
Make numbers from coloured ▲ and flavoured marzipan to correlate to the relevant birthday, or as an imaginative gift for a child who is learning to count.

·52·

Mechanical tints When first specifying the tint, always give percentages of the process colors, which can be obtained from a tint chart, rather than giving a Pantone color swatch or reference number to match, as many special colors cannot be obtained from the four-color process. The tint on the proof can then be checked against the tint chart. Watch out for mottled tints, which can be caused by the film or plate being exposed out of contact. Look also for moiré.

Register Check registration marks to see if the job has been proofed in register. If it is correct, all you will see is black. If it is out of register, one or more colors will show next to the black.

Trim and bleed Check trim marks for position and that the bleed allowance is correct.

"Flopping" When a picture appears reversed left to right in a color proof, it should be marked "flop." This correction is not simply a matter of the color house turning the film over, as the emulsion would be on the wrong side and therefore out of contact with the plate. Instead, a new contact film has to be made so that the emulsion is on the right side.

Fit If the register marks fit, but you can see colors sticking out from the edge of the picture (right), the job has been planned out of fit.

Always check the following:

1 Register

2 Trim and bleed

3 Sizes – if a grid is used, check proof against it

4 Type – broken, missing, illegible, too fine

5 Color – check the color bar

6 Flopped subjects

7 Artwork overlays

8 Tints

9 Special colors

10 Returns – check that color house has sent back all artwork and color transparencies originally supplied

11 Gutter

• CERAMIC DISH •
With a little searching glass or ceramic dishes can be found to match up to all manner of hobbies and interests – a fish would be suitable for an aquarium enthusiast.

• GARDEN GNOME •
Ideal for the gardener. Fill the barrow with sweets that the gardener can suck or chew whilst pondering over his garden or, recovering from strenuous digging. ►

• INITIALS •
◄ *Decorate sweets with letters formed from fondant or marzipan or piped chocolate and arrange them in a box so they spell out the recipient's name or a message.*

• ARTISTS PALETTE •
◄ *Coloured sweets provide instant, edible splashes of colour and – hopefully – inspiration for a work of art.*

FOR THE SWEET-TOOTHED COOK •
Combine practicality with indulgence for the sweet-toothed cook – give equipment that is needed for making sweets, a selection of sweets to illustrate just how delicious homemade ones can be, plus a copy of this book.

▲ • WATCH •
Sweets are a timeless gift, when teamed with a watch that will act as a lasting memory of the care and trouble that lay behind the giving of the gift.

What are the rules for marking up proofs?

THE ANSWER to this question depends to a large extent on how much technical knowledge the designer has. The following pages look specifically at checking size, crop, position, etc., but it is the way the designer marks up color corrections that is crucial to a successful finished result.

If the designer does not have in-depth technical knowledge of reproduction, it is much better to state the result required, rather than tell the color separation house how to achieve it. For example, if the proof has an area of green that is lighter than the green on the transparency, the instruction "Make this green darker – see original" is sufficient to tell the color house what needs doing. Telling the color house *how* to do the correction would involve saying "increase cyan," possibly even mentioning by what percentage the cyan should be increased. However, color correction is an area where a little knowledge is a dangerous thing. In the example above, the designer may not know enough to realize that the cyan strength is correct, but it is the yellow that needs to be reduced.

For most designers then, the correction of color consists of marking up the proofs where the color is not sufficiently close to the original and saying in what way it differs. It is not enough to say "Reproof – see original"; you must indicate to the color separation house in what way you think the proof differs.

The designer should not write a little essay about the proof, such as "The trees look a somewhat darker green than the transparency, but the blue in the river should not be any lighter and the sky is correct," but specify "Lighten green in trees." If a proof is nearly correct, it is best to accept it.

Where a reproof is required, this should be stated clearly. Knowing when to ask for reproofs is a matter of experience, but as a general rule, if the proof is so far away from the original that you are worried that it may still not be correct after correction, then a reproof is justified.

STANDARD COLOR CORRECTION MARKS

These symbols are not often used, but can be useful if the designer has the technical knowledge to mark up proofs in this way. It probably involves knowing how to use a densitometer, and how to read color bars.

The instruction "improve detail and modeling" refers to the highlights and details that need enhancing. Hardness and softness are the terms used to describe whether the edges of a color, shape, or tone are either too sharp or too indistinct.

If an image is out of register, the films for one or more of the four colors have been misaligned. If the edges of the image are not in register, the film has been positioned incorrectly on the plate. "Slur" refers to a proofing defect which elongates the halftone dots.

Instruction	Marginal mark
1 Passed for press	
2 Reproof	
3 Reduce contrast	
4 Increase contrast	
5 Improve detail or modeling	
6 Too hard, make softer	U
7 Too soft, make sharper	∧
8 Rectify uneven tint	
9 Repair broken type, rule or tint	X
10 Improve register	
11 Correct slur	

Process color	Increase	Reduce
Yellow	Y+	Y–
Magenta	M+	M–
Cyan	C+	C–
Black	B+	B–

CORRECT

TOO MUCH CONTRAST

TOO LITTLE CONTRAST

This gives some idea of how many different faults a proof can have. The errors in all these pictures are only slight, but the slightest difference can change a picture entirely. All of these faults are described in more detail later.

LOSS OF DETAIL

DETAIL TOO HARD

DETAIL TOO SOFT

TOO MUCH CYAN

TOO MUCH MAGENTA

TOO MUCH YELLOW

TOO LITTLE CYAN

TOO LITTLE MAGENTA

TOO LITTLE YELLOW

How should I go about making my marks?

Marking up a proof When marking up a proof, write clear, concise instructions – any misunderstanding can result in more work and cost. Keep comments well spaced; also it is a good idea to use different-colored permanent pens to correspond to each color correction. Distinguish between mistakes that you feel are the fault of the color house and those that are the designer's. Take care to get corrections right at first color proof stage, as corrections at second color proof stage may require rescanning, which is costly and time-consuming. It is

(handwritten annotations on proof):

TYPE OUT OF REGISTER

Background colour too dark. Lighten overall —Y —C

Ⓐ New copy to strip-in. See bromide attached

Too much loss of detail in dark areas. Improve definition

Sky too red/warm —M overall

Dusk at Koh Samui

erience

Travel Information

Flying Time: 13-16 hours
Distance: 5,960 miles
Local Time: GMT +7 hours

Thai International flights - SUN (non-stop), MON, TUE, THUR, FRI and SAT (all direct), from **London Heathrow** by Boeing 747 scheduled service overnight to Bangkok. Return flights leave Bangkok on a SAT (non-stop), SUN, MON, WED, THUR and FRI (all direct). Flying overnight to the UK.
Business Class and Royal Orchid Class available.

Flights are also available with **Philippine Airlines** - overnight on a MON and Wed with return to the UK TUE from London Gatwick returning to the UK overnight on a MON and Wed. Flights are available on request.

Tourist Information, contact
For further information, contact
Tourism Authority of Thailand,
49 Albemarle Street, London, W1X 1FE
Tel. (01) 499 7679

Visa and Health Requirements
Innoculation against typhoid and tetanus is recommended, and you should consider protection about taking the appropriate malaria tablets. You should hygiene are reasonably high in Thailand, but you should not drink tap water and should be cautious about eating raw vegetables.

Daily Sunshine (hours)	Monthly Rainfall (inches)
9.0	0.3
9.0	1.0
8.5	2.5
8.5	2.5
5.5	6.5
5.5	6.5
5.0	7.5
5.0	12.5
5.0	8.5
7.0	8.5
8.5	0.3

ate figures are hand on Bangkok

Handwritten annotations:
- CHECK REGISTER!
- This symbol must print red 100% M 100% Y
- Artwork overlays out of fit see original artwork.
- improve whites of clouds
- Black tint shadows look too dark. Please check against other pages to make consistent

"James Bond Island", Phuket

9

Market Day, Bangkok

not always necessary for a reproof to be proofed in the same way as the first proof. For example, the first proof may be a wet proof of which several sets have been done, but a Cromalin may suffice for the reproof and will be cheaper. If the change concerns only size or position and not color, the reproof can be a blueprint.

AVOIDING AMBIGUOUS INSTRUCTIONS

If you are not sure how to achieve the result you want, speak to the color house before you mark up the proof. If you lack experience they will be very willing to help you.

brighten colours

This instruction is not specific enough; does the designer mean lighten the colors, add more color, or improve contrast?

—improve magenta

If the designer gives this instruction on a color proof the color house is left wondering whether the instruction is to minus magenta or improve magenta. The ambiguity lies in the fact that a handwritten minus sign can be mistaken for a dash.

see transparency

This type of instruction is not so much ambiguous as non-committal. As much as possible, the designer should always specify what is actually *wrong* with the proof. To say "See transparency" without any qualifications is simply sloppy.

looks too warm

Does the designer mean the proof looks too magenta or too yellow?

make greener

What color green is greener? With this instruction does the designer mean emerald green, pea green, lime green, sage green, bottle green, leaf green...? This type of ambiguity can occur with any color.

improve quality

Another woolly instruction which will have the color house wondering what the designer means – is the instruction referring to the films not matching, the color density not being right or one or all of the colors being overdone?

you haven't caught the mood of this shot

An instruction guaranteed to irritate. The scanner operator does not have a "mood" button. The operator will have matched the transparency unless a specific other instruction was given on the layout.

What is a good black and white halftone?

A GOOD BLACK AND WHITE original should be sharp and have reasonable contrast. Although the separator can increase contrast, it is always easier to start with an original with a good density range. When reproduced, a good black and white original will have a pin dot in the highlight areas and just stay open enough in the shadows to hold detail, while being heavy enough to make a good strong black.

With a bad black and white reproduction, the proof could either show the highlight dot as too large, making the picture look flat, or too small, making the whites blown out and coarse. If it is the shadow areas that are wrong, it will either be because the shadow setting is too low, resulting in the shadow areas being too light and gray, or because it is too high, so that filling in occurs.

This picture has too much contrast and has lost detail. The highlights have dropped out, losing the detail on the tie; the shadows have filled in, resulting in loss of texture on the jacket.

This picture is too flat: the whites look gray, and the shadows are gray instead of black. The overall effect is insipid.

A good black and white picture should be sharp, crisp, and punchy (left). There should be a very small dot on the highlights for detail, but it should carry enough weight to look black. Using a glass (below) to look at the good halftones reveals that the contrast is set correctly with good white highlights appearing on the watch.

LOSS OF DETAIL

FLAT HALFTONE

GOOD BLACK AND WHITE HALFTONE

What is good black and white line repro?

A GOOD black and white line original should have clean, strong areas of black. Where the lines are very fine or broken, the original may have to be treated as a halftone or a line and tone combination. This is often the case with old line engravings, where the lines are so fine and close together that line reproduction will lose detail by making the darker areas solid.

If you want to give a colored effect to the picture, you can add a flat tint such as yellow to give the effect of antique paper (below).

LINE AND 10% TINT

4-COLOR LINE

GOOD BLACK AND WHITE LINE

With a good black and white line shot (left), you should check that the shadows have not filled in and that the very fine lines in the highlights are printing. If either of these is wrong, ask the color house to re-shoot them. It is very difficult to reproduce these line shots as four-color, as the tones are so thin that it is nearly impossible to register the colors exactly (far left).

With some pictures, especially those with type, it is possible to shoot the three colors (cyan, magenta, and yellow) conventionally, then to shoot a line of the black, which is combined with the normal black tone. It gives greater definition to the picture and type; but check the price with the color house first, as it is likely to be expensive. This postcard (above) was proofed with a combination of tone and black line. As the close-up through the glass shows, the black line is crisp and sharp.

What is a good duotone?

IT IS A MISTAKE for a designer to think that a poor black and white original can be improved by reproducing it as a duotone, since all it will make is a poor duotone.

A true duotone is produced when two halftone films of the same subject are printed in different colors. The heavier color (usually black) has a 45° screen angle and is reproduced to full range, with dots from 5% to 95%. The second, lighter color is at a different angle and is usually heavier in the highlights, with a range of 15% to 95%. The designer may not want the full range of the lighter color and could ask for it to print at only 60% strength, giving a range of 2% to 60%. This can be difficult to visualize, and the designer should discuss it with the color separation house and look at examples of similar previous jobs.

With some high-quality black and white work, such as photography books, duotones are reproduced so as to look like black and whites and use a very pale gray as the second color. This can give very good results. The gray brings out the midtones – giving more body to the printed piece.

Another way to reproduce a black and white picture in two colors is to print a black and white halftone in black on a percentage tint panel of a second color. This is sometimes wrongly described as a duotone. It will result in less depth and detail than a true duotone.

GOOD DUOTONE

FLAT DUOTONE

10% DUOTONE

30% DUOTONE

B + W HALFTONE AND FLAT TINT

50% DUOTONE

70% DUOTONE

The pictures on this spread show some of the different effects you can achieve with duotones. On the opposite page, the top image is full strength, while the bottom one looks flat and uninteresting. The block of four shown left shows different strengths of the cyan, from the very subtle 10%, which gives just a touch of blue to the highlights, to three-quarters strength. The halftone with a flat cyan tint (above) looks flat compared with the real thing.

The moiré picture (below) shows what can happen when both colors are at the same screen angle.

MOIRE

What is a good four-color black/sepia?

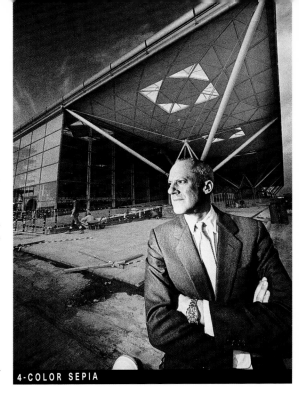

4-COLOR SEPIA

WITH THE USE of scanners making the practice more economical, a lot of designers now use four-color black and whites. These give a very strong black and good detail. They also allow very subtle shades of color to come through, instead of just gray, black or white.

The originals are scanned just as if they were color originals, and it is possible to run a particular color stronger to give, for example, a red tinge to a black and white photo, although this will need to be discussed with the color separation house. The balance of the colors depends on the requirements of the designer.

Sepia effects Sepias come in many different shades, so for the best result always supply the color house with a tear-sheet of the result you require (left). Tear-sheets can be taken from magazines and publications. A three-color sepia effect can look as effective as a four-color version, and the former is cheaper to print (right top and bottom).

3-COLOR SEPIA

COOL BLACK

4-COLOR SPECIAL BLACK

WARM BLACK

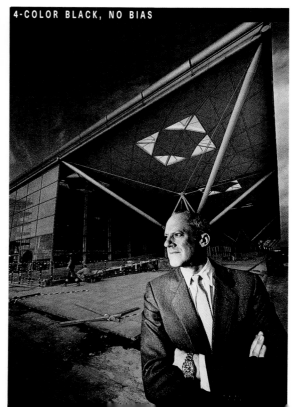

4-COLOR BLACK, NO BIAS

In the first picture (far left) the cyan is slightly above the magenta and yellow, giving a cool effect. This seems to work well with pictures of machinery, giving a modern look. The warm picture (below left) has the magenta as the predominant color, giving a sepia-like effect. The neutral picture (below right) has all the colors in the correct balance, but allows subtle shades to come through. In the special effect (above right) the magenta is printed in negative, giving pink highlights and greenish shadows.

Remember that although the color house can reproduce a color transparency to print as black and white, it cannot convert a color transparency to four-color black, as the scanner can reproduce only it as full color. The solution is to make a black and white print from the transparency and reproduce it as four-color black.

How do I know if the proof is too flat?

If the job looks flat overall, this can be caused either by the highlight dots being set too big or by the dot in the shadow being set too small (right). If the highlight dots are too big, the whites will appear slightly gray. If the shadow dots are too small, the black will not come out strong enough, and all the shadows will need to be increased.

If the proof lacks punch and none of the colors seem bright enough, then the shadows are too open, and they and the midtones should be increased.

FLAT PROOF

FINAL PROOF

Identifying the problem Here you can see a large dot of cyan on the reds, making the picture dirty (above). To be correct, the cyan dot should be as fine as possible. The proof is too flat and has been scanned incorrectly, with the highlight dot set too big and the shadow dot set too small. To correct the picture, you will have to rescan it. Compared with the final proof (center), the highlights are gray instead of white, all the colors look dirty, and the shadows are gray instead of black.

How do I know if the proof is too weak?

WEAK PROOF

To check whether the proof is too weak, have a look at all the tints on the job. If these are too light, it is likely that the proof has been run with too little ink on one or more colors. The color subjects will look thin, and the black shadow areas will appear slightly gray, with the midtones also thin (left).

If the tints are correct but the color subjects look thin, they may have been scanned incorrectly. If you do not have a densitometer, ask the color house to read the ink densities and mark them on the proof.

Checking the color bar Viewed through a linen tester, the color bar shows a weak proof of the 40% dot of the cyan, which is only half strength (right). The 80% is also below strength. This tells you that the film is correct,

but the proof has been run with too little cyan.

This proof (above) is weak. The fault lies either with the proofing or the scanning, and checking the color bar will tell you which is at fault. Here, the scanning is

incorrect, with the highlight dots and shadow dots both set too small. The whites on the paint tubes have lost all the detail, the shadows look gray rather than black, and all the colors look very pale.

How do I know if the highlights are poor?

Here, the highlight dots have been set too small on scanning, which has caused a loss of detail in the lighter areas (right). As a result, all the pastel colors look thin.

This has also affected the complementary colors that give modeling, such as the cyan on the red flowers, which lack definition and shape. It is not caused by proofing, as that would not affect the smaller dots to such an extent.

POOR HIGHLIGHTS

FINAL PROOF

Identifying the problem
Looking at part of the proof through a linen tester shows that the highlight dots are too small. If they were increased, they would stand out from the white paper areas, giving more definition in

the highlights. The darker reds should have a small cyan dot for modeling, also.

How do I know if the proof is too dense?

DENSE PROOF

This proof is too dense (left). If it is caused by the ink, the 40% and 80% steps will have filled in. If these are correct, it is a fault in reproduction. Here, all the colors look too strong: the red flowers have gone brown, the yellows are orange, and the whites look gray.

Checking the color bar If the proof carries too much ink, the three-color neutral will look too dark – nearly black instead of dark gray.

50% 40% 80% 80% 80% 40% C M B

How do I know if the proof is up or down on cyan?

If a proof is up on the cyan, the three-color gray will have a blue cast. To see if this is caused by the magenta and yellow being down, check the 40% and 80% cyan steps on the color bar. If they have filled in, the proof is up on cyan. If these are correct, the fault is in the reproduction.

Here, the whites and grays have a blue cast, the yellows look green, the pinks in the fabric is too dirty, and the red flowers are going brown.

Checking the color bar You can see that the cyan 80% step has filled in and looks the same as the 100% step next to it (right). This shows that the proof has too much cyan ink.

Identifying the problem When a proof is down on cyan, there is virtually no cyan dot in the enlarged area (left).

If a proof is down on the cyan, the three-color gray on the color bar will appear brown. To see if this is caused by the magenta and yellow being up, check the 40% and 80% cyan steps on the color bar. If they are open, the proof is down on cyan. If these are correct, the fault is in the reproduction.

In this picture, the blues in the fabric look thin and warm, the red flowers have lost all their modeling, and the grays also look warm.

Checking the color bar You can see that the 40% step has nearly disappeared (left), which shows that the proofing, and not the separation, is at fault.

How do I know if the proof is up or down on magenta?

If a proof is up on the magenta, the three-color gray will have a pink cast. To see if this is caused by the cyan and yellow being down, check the 40% and 80% magenta steps on the color bar. If they have filled in, the proof is up on magenta. If these are correct, the fault is in the reproduction.

Here, (right) the pinks in the fabric look too strong, the greens look dirty, the yellows are going orange, and all the neutrals in the fabric look pink.

UP ON MAGENTA

FINAL PROOF

Checking the color bar You can see that the 40% step is too strong, being nearer 60%, and that the 80% step has filled in solid, showing that the proof has too much magenta ink.

Identifying the problem There should be a small dot of magenta on the darker greens to give them modeling and definition.

DOWN ON MAGENTA

If a proof is down on the magenta, the three-color gray (below) on the color bar will appear green. To see if this is caused by the cyan and yellow being up, check the 40% and 80% cyan steps on the color bar. If they are open, the proof is down on magenta. If these are correct, the fault is in the reproduction.

In this picture (left), the grays in the fabric look green, the greens on the flowers have lost all their modeling, the reds look orange, and the pinks look thin.

Checking the color bar This shows the green bias on the three-color neutral step (right). The magenta dot should be only slightly smaller than the cyan dot.

How do I know if the proof is up or down on yellow?

If a proof is up on the yellow, the three-color gray will have a yellow cast. To see if this is caused by the cyan and magenta being down, check the 40% and 80% yellow steps on the color bar. If they have filled in, the proof is up on yellow. If these are correct, the fault is in the reproduction.

Here, (right) the neutrals in the picture have a yellow cast, the lighter yellows and greens in the fabric all look too strong, and the reds are slightly orange.

UP ON YELLOW

FINAL PROOF

Checking the color bar
Although the yellow is difficult to see, being such a light color, this shows the 80% step filling in (right).

80%   40%

50% 40% 80%   80% 40% 50%

50% 40% 80%   80%

Identifying the problem
Looking at part of the proof through a glass shows the blacks looking mauve; the green leaf has half the yellow required, and there is no yellow dot in the highlight (left).

If a proof is down on yellow, the three-color gray on the color bar will appear mauve. To see if this is caused by the cyan and magenta being up, check the 40% and 80% yellow steps on the color bar. If they are open, the proof is down on yellow. If these are correct, the fault is in the reproduction.

In this picture (left), the neutral grays are mauve, the yellows are too weak, the reds look pink, and the greens appear thin and too blue.

Checking the color bar Here you can see the obvious mauve cast in the three-color neutral step, showing the lack of yellow ink.

How do I know if the proof is up or down on black?

If a proof is up on the black, check either the 40% and 80% steps on the color bar to see if they have filled in, or the black on the progressives, if they are available. It can be difficult to see this fault on the proof.

Here (right), there is some loss of detail in the shadows, the gray highlights on the side of the paint brushes have started to disappear, and some areas, such as the flowers and neutrals in the fabric, look dirty.

UP ON BLACK

FINAL PROOF

Checking the color bar Through a glass you can see that the 80% step has filled in and that the 40% looks too strong. The proof is carrying too much black ink.

80% 40%

Identifying the problem The black dot on the darker brown is far too small (above). If it were increased to double the size, it would increase the contrast with the lighter brown, which would still not be carrying a black dot.

Here, (left) the shadows in the picture look gray instead of black, and the red flowers and brown of the palette have both lost detail.

If a proof is down on the black, the 40% and 80% steps on the color bar will look open. Use a linen tester to check this on the color bar below.

80% 40% 50%

50% 40% 80% 80% 40% 50% C M

Color proof correction: fashion and beauty

FIRST PROOF

There are several points that need attention on fashion shots. White fabrics need to be as white as possible, but hold enough to give detail. Black fabrics should be as black as possible, but still be open enough to give detail. It can be difficult to match a fabric – try to supply a swatch of the material to the color house.

First proof Here, the black dress has filled in, losing detail (**1**); the flesh looks sore (**2**); the white dress looks pink (**3**); and there is also a loss of detail on the red dress (**4**).

Instruction to separator
Reduce magenta overall; clean up whites; hold detail in black and red dresses.

First proof variations (Above right) Too much yellow makes the highlights look creamy, the blue dress green, and the flesh tones too orange.
(Right) Too much cyan makes the highlights and grays blue. The blue dress is filled in, losing detail in the darker areas. The black dress has a blue cast.
(Below right) Too much black makes the black dress and the bows on the blue dress fill in. The shadows on the knees have filled in. Where there is too much black, it can be difficult to tell, so look at the progressives.
(Bottom right) This generally

weak reproduction shows the highlights disappearing, losing some of the modeling on the white dress. The black dress looks gray.

Identifying the problem The enlargement shows the predominance of magenta dots. On a neutral highlight area like this, the cyan should be larger than the magenta dots, and the yellow (although difficult to see) should be the same as the magenta.

FINAL PROOF

With a reduction in the magenta, the white dress has lost its pink cast; the flesh looks natural; the black dress has opened out, letting more modeling come through; and the black has been increased slightly on the red dress to help the modeling.

It is better to use black rather than cyan to improve the modeling, as cyan would dirty the red rather than darken it.

Where you want a subject cut out, as here, it is much easier for the color house if it is on a light background, as this makes it easier to mask around the required image area.

TOO YELLOW

TOO CYAN

TOO BLACK

GENERALLY WEAK

Color proof correction: skin tones

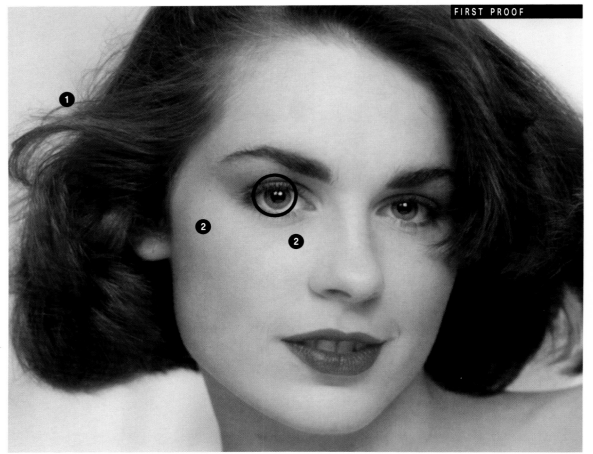

FIRST PROOF

With skin tones, the color house has to take care to get the right color balance, as the slightest imbalance can change the picture entirely.

The problem to watch out for with hair is not so much color (since all hair is different) but fit. Because hair consists of thousands of tiny strands, good fit is vital, so the transparency needs to be as sharp as possible.

First proof is flat and un-sharp. The hair has lost detail (**1**); the flesh has lost detail and is soft (**2**).

Instruction to separator Too soft; reduce cyan; improve whites and highlights on eyes.

First proof variations (Top right) The magenta is up, but only in the midtones and shadows. The lighter areas of the flesh are correct, but it becomes sore in the stronger areas. Also, the blue of the eyes is slightly mauve. (Above right) This looks flat. The darker flesh tones are the right color, but there is no difference between them and the lighter areas, which are too full.
(Below right) The picture is down in yellow. If you reduced the magenta, the face would lose all its color, so the yellow has to be increased instead.
(Bottom right) This is down in magenta. Reducing the yellow would make the face too pale.

Identifying the problem You can tell the picture is flat by checking the catchlights in the eyes. In a well-reproduced picture, they are paper white, rather than carrying a dot. The same applies to teeth.

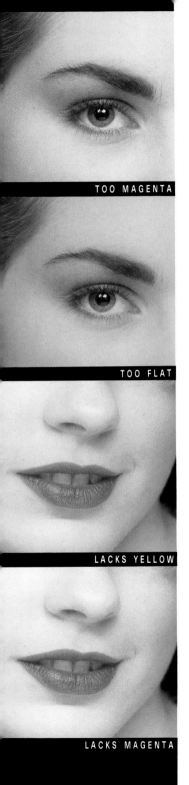

TOO MAGENTA

TOO FLAT

LACKS YELLOW

LACKS MAGENTA

Final proof The importance of the sharpness of the picture is seen below. The detail in the hair has been improved – individual hairs now stand out – as has the skin. The highlights on the lips make them appear glossy.

The white highlights in the eyes have dropped, showing that the tonal range is correct. This has also allowed some of the more subtle colors in the background to come through.

FINAL PROOF

Color proof correction: skin tones

FIRST PROOF

Identifying the problem Using a linen tester to enlarge part of the proof shows that the highlights on the chrome are dropping out, but the next tones are also losing highlights in the complementary colors, causing a loss of detail.

First proof This has excessive contrast and generally needs the highlights increased overall. (It is better to give a general instruction rather than to request increases in the individual colors – cyan on fleshes; magenta on yellow; magenta and black on greens; and so on.) The exaggerated contrast has over-emphasized the subtle colors of the fleshes (**1**), making the yellows too strong (**2**) and the pinks too magenta (**3**).

Instruction to separator Reduce contrast overall.

First proof variations (Right)
This has too much yellow – the flesh has turned yellow, the slight shadow on the underside of the ball has a yellow cast, and the shirt color is too strong.
(Far right) This is too flat, losing detail in the hat and flesh tones. Also, the ball looks gray instead of white.

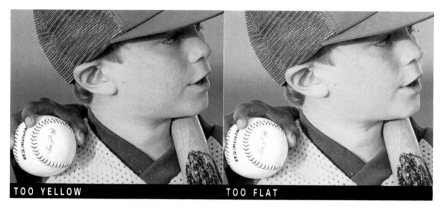

TOO YELLOW   TOO FLAT

Final proof With the contrast reduced, the picture becomes less garish. The modeling on the faces and green shirts has been improved, although there has been a slight loss of the exaggerated detail in the highlights, such as the writing on the ball.

FINAL PROOF

Color proof correction: food

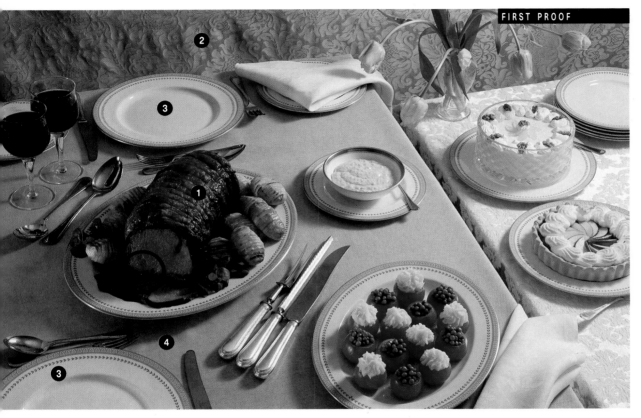

FIRST PROOF

Food is one of the most difficult subjects to reproduce, and your instructions to the color house should be exact. Let them know which is the most important part of the shot. If, as here, it is the candles, they can then exaggerate the highlight detail, which in turn slightly decreases the midtone detail of the roast.

The food should look appetizing without being too garish. (Meat, for example, can easily look sore and bloody if carrying too much magenta, or pale and insipid if the colors are slightly out of balance.) The most difficult aspect of food reproduction is accurately representing items with subtle or very little color. Foods that are difficult to reproduce include parsnips, potatoes, and dairy produce, whereas peas, carrots, and bananas, for example, are much easier, as they have strong, identifiable colors. Making sure that the colors do not look false is sometimes more important than matching the transparency exactly.

First proof The cyan is too strong overall, causing the top of the roast to look too brown and dirty (**1**); the neutral lace background has a greenish cast (**2**); the neutral grays on the plates are slightly blue (**3**); and the green tablecloth is much too strong (**4**); since the whites and light, creamy colors are correct, it is probably only the midtones that are out of balance.

Instruction to separator
Reduce cyan.

Identifying the problem Using a linen tester shows that the blue dots are too large.

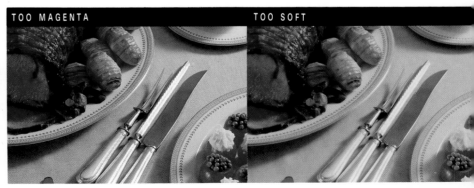

TOO MAGENTA

TOO SOFT

Final proof With the highlights increased, the large white areas have disappeared, and both the detail and the texture of the ice cream have been improved. It is difficult to remove all the casts from a white subject, and in this case, the blue in the background gives the ice cream a blue cast.

FINAL PROOF

TOO CYAN   TOO YELLOW   TOO MAGENTA

First proof variations (Far left) This has cyan bias, making the greens too strong. The oranges and reds on the cookie have gone brown, and the yellow looks slightly green.
(Center left) This is up in yellow, making the reds on the cookie orange and the ice cream yellow.
(Left) This is too magenta; the ice cream is beginning to turn mauve, the green dirty, and the red edge on the cookie looks sore.

Color proof correction: landscapes

When a sky looks dirty, it is often due to too much yellow. If this is reduced, the sky becomes clearer but slightly lighter. If you increase the cyan and magenta, the sky becomes bluer but darker.

First proof In this case, the picture is too flat overall, making the clouds look dirty and gray (**1**). If the highlight dots are made smaller, it will also help the definition between the beiges (**2**) and greens (**3**). This is done by reducing the cyan highlights in the beige and the magenta highlights in the green.

Instruction to separator
Brighten highlights.

FIRST PROOF

Identifying the problem The enlargement shows the highlight in the clouds. The magenta and yellow dots should be as small as possible, with the cyan dots only slightly bigger. Here, they are all too big.

First proof variations (Below left) With the yellow slightly down, the gray rocks look mauve and the clouds have mauve edges. Reducing the cyan and magenta would only make the picture look thin.

(Below right) The lack of

YELLOW DOWN

MAGENTA DOWN

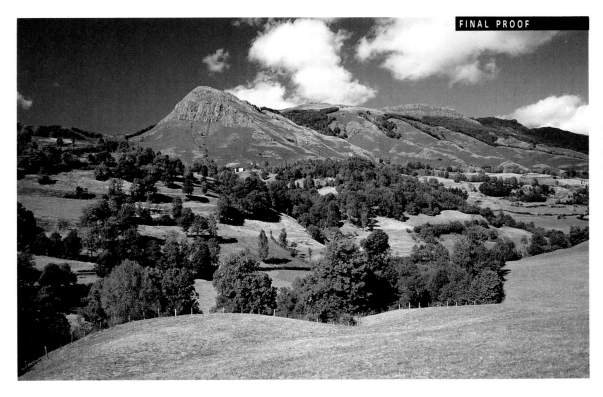

FINAL PROOF

Final proof Here, the color balance is the same as the first proof, but the range of the picture has been increased by making the highlight dots smaller. This has made the picture look much sharper, with greater detail and definition.

magenta has given the sky a green cast. In fact, all the greens are too strong.
(Below left) The greens are all too

heavy and the sky is too dark, so ask for the cyan and the yellow to be reduced.
(Below right) Although the color

balance is correct, there is not enough difference between the dark greens and the shadows, so the black should be increased.

TOO CYAN AND YELLOW   **BLACK DOWN**

Color proof correction: landscapes

Grass and foliage can be difficult subjects to reproduce correctly. The predominant colors are obviously cyan and yellow, but the balance between them needs to be just right – there is a danger that the subject can become too blue or yellow.

Magenta is also important, as it helps to give detail, but too much of it will make the grass or foliage dirty and brown. If you want the grass to be darker, but not to become dirty, increase the black. Increasing the black will also help foliage with dark reds, mauves, browns, and blues in its coloring. It makes the foliage darker without affecting the general color.

FIRST PROOF

Identifying the problem The enlargement shows that the large cyan dots on the pink flowers are killing the magenta, so making them dull. Reducing cyan will let the magenta come through.

First proof The cyan is too strong, giving everything a cyan cast (**1**) and killing all the fine detail in the greens (**2**). Increasing the other colors will only lose more detail.

Instruction to separator
Reduce cyan.

112

Final proof The only difference to the first proof here is a reduction of cyan. As a result, detail has been improved and the modeling on the foliage is clearer, allowing more colors to come through.

The stones in the pool now look a warm brown and the whites on the building are neutral. The best way of telling if any of the colors are out of balance is to look at the neutral gray, such as the rocks in this picture.

FINAL PROOF

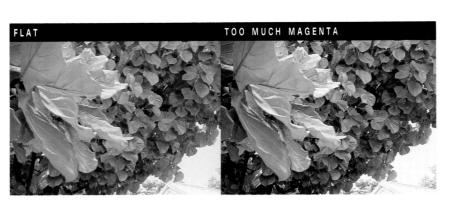

FLAT

TOO MUCH MAGENTA

First proof variations (Far left) This picture is flat and lifeless. The sky is gray rather than white and has dots of all colors, and the details in the leaves have lost all their crispness.

(Left) Here, the magenta is too strong. The sky has a pink cast, the darker leaves are slightly mauve, and the light greens are looking brown and dirty.

Color proof correction: landscapes

In general, clients are not too worried about matching travel shots with the original so long as the printed result is a bright, appealing picture. It is important to tell the color house if you want to improve on the original, otherwise they will attempt to match it.

First proof Even if this proof matches the original, it is not suitable for a travel brochure – the beach looks dirty (**1**); the clouds look dull (**2**); the sky is not blue (**3**); and the greens are too dark and lack detail (**4**).

Identifying the problem This enlargement shows dots in the white sail. These should be dropped out to make the sail whiter, and therefore stand out from the background.

Instruction to separator Make less dense; brighten overall.

FIRST PROOF

First proof variation (Right) This shows the improvement on the skintones, which looked sore and sunburned on the first proof. The girl's top might be the wrong color, but it is not a critical error.

SKINTONES IMPROVED

OVER-CORRECTED

First proof variation (Left) This has been over-corrected. The clouds now look thin and the sky looks gray, or even slightly green, instead of blue.

FINAL PROOF

Final proof This shows a big improvement on the first proof. The whole shot is more attractive, with far more detail in the foliage, and the clouds look whiter and more detailed.

Color proof correction: landscapes

FIRST PROOF

First proof On skiing shots, the snow can present quite a problem. Snow is not paper white, and when reproducing, as it always has a reflected color, and when reproducing, it can be difficult to make the snow white enough while keeping a big enough dot to keep the snow's detail. In this case, the highlight dots have been set too small, causing the snow to disappear to paper white.

Instruction to separator Snow is disappearing to paper white; increase detail.

Identifying the problem In the enlargement below you can see that there are no dots at all in the snow.

First proof variations (Left)
Here the shadows are too
strong, causing a loss of detail in
all the dark areas.

(Left) Detail has also been lost on
this proof, but in the highlights.
This has made the
complementary colors that give
detail on the red and yellow to be
too low, thus losing the modeling.

(Left) This is down on the yellow
and also slightly weak. The snow
has a slight blue/violet cast,
there is a loss of detail, and the
shadows have gone too mauve.

FINAL PROOF

Final proof With stronger
highlights, the modeling on the
snow has been improved, as it
has on the clothing.

Color proof correction: cars

The special colors (which are sometimes metallic) used on the paintwork of cars can be difficult to match using four colors.

To get the maximum detail on the molding of the car body and lights, the scanner operator needs to set the scanner on the car, which sometimes means sacrificing the background.

It is vital that the transparencies for car photographs be pin sharp. If an image is not sharp enough, reproduction cannot hold the detail; the color house can do nothing to improve it.

First proof This looks soft (**1**), losing the modeling on the white car especially (**2**). The cars have a yellow bias, which makes them look dull (**3**).

Instruction to separator
Reduce yellow; improve fit; retouch shadows to give soft edges.

Identifying the problem In the magnified image above you can see the importance of fit. The magenta is out of fit, making the picture look soft and blurred.

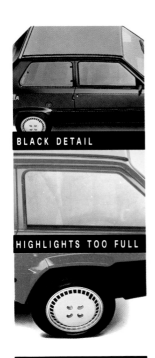

BLACK DETAIL

HIGHLIGHTS TOO FULL

TOO YELLOW

First proof variations (Top) Here, the shadows are too full. (Middle) In this case, the highlights are too full, causing a loss of detail in the interior of the car.
(Bottom) This picture is too yellow. The reds have gone slightly orange and the chromes look warm.

Final proof With a reduction of the yellow and the general sharpening of the image, the modeling and definition in the bodywork have been improved. The shadows under the cars have been retouched to give soft edges. When shadows are cut out on white, they look better if reproduced only in black. There is some moiré patterning on the hood grilles, which is unavoidable.

Color proof correction: cars

First proof This picture has been taken under a yellow awning causing all the reflections on the car to appear too yellow (**1**). The designer should have asked the color house to reduce this, but without this request, they assumed that they should follow the transparency. It now has to be altered at proof stage, and would therefore be an "author's correction," chargeable to the client.

When reproducing chrome, the best results are achieved by dropping the highlights out to paper white. This has been done here, but has affected the rest of the picture by causing the whites above the car to lose some of their detail.

Instruction to separator
Reduce yellow.

FIRST PROOF

Identifying the problem
Looking at an area of the proof through a linen tester shows that the highlights on the chrome have dropped out to white. If there were any dots in the chrome, it would look dull and flat.

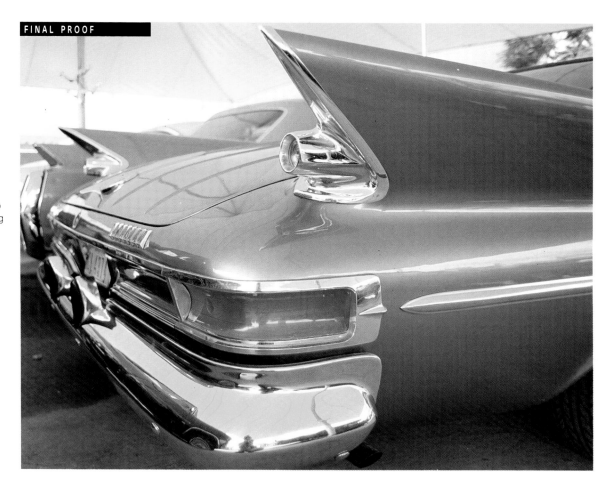

Final proof With the overall predominance of yellow now reduced, the car looks more natural. Here, the browns and beiges have lost some yellow and look more natural. This also allows more detail and modeling to come through.

TOO SOFT   TOO MAGENTA   ALL COLORS WEAK

First proof variations (Far left) The softness has made the highlights on the red light look fuzzy and un-sharp. The red tones on the yellow have virtually disappeared.
(Center left) Too much magenta has made the yellows take on an orange hue. The brown looks too warm, and the shadow detail in the red light is disappearing.
(Left) Although the color balance in the brown is correct here, the overall weakness of color makes the picture look too light. This has also meant that the fine lines in the yellow are disappearing.

Color proof correction: interiors

Furniture can be difficult to reproduce, as a slight imbalance of any color can change the shade of the wood entirely.

First proof This picture is badly lit, with the top being too light (**1**) while the bottom is in shadow (**2**). The highlight dot needs to be set slightly bigger, but not so much as to lose detail. The proof is also down on the magenta, making the wood too yellow (**3**) and garish

FIRST PROOF

Identifying the problem The lines on the wood are short of magenta, causing the wood to lose its texture and detail (above). The cyan dot in the darker areas is too small because the picture has too much contrast.

Instruction to separator
Reduce highlights; increase magenta.

Final proof With slightly larger dots in the highlights, the detail in the top half and lighter areas of the picture has been improved, and the modeling of the wood is much better. Reducing the cyan and yellow shadow while increasing the magenta slightly has made the bottom half of the picture less dense and slightly warmer.

FINAL PROOF

TOO MUCH CONTRAST

SHADOWS FILLED IN

First proof variations (Top) This has too much contrast – the highlights have dropped out, losing all detail.
(Above) The magenta has been increased, but the cyan and yellow shadows are too heavy, which has filled in the darker areas.

Color proof correction: interiors

The main problem with a white subject is that it often looks flat and uninteresting. Very little detail or modeling comes across. Any slight imbalance of color can cause a cast, and shadows falling across the subject will have a color cast. Using an increased black can give more shape and modeling. Take care with backlit subjects such as this one, as they have false highlights.

First proof The black here is too strong, causing everything to look black (**1**) and dirty (**2**).

Instruction to separator
Reduce black; lighten highlights.

FIRST PROOF

Identifying the problem Using a linen tester to examine the proof shows the black dots on the red making the picture look dull.

Final proof This shows a reduction in the black. Also the color house has lightened the highlights by making a slight reduction in the highlight dot of the other colors to compensate for the backlighting.

The reduction in the black has allowed the richness in the red floor tiles and the stools to come through. You can now see that the handles on the units are red; they were previously obscured by too much black.

FINAL PROOF

TOO YELLOW AND CYAN

WEAK OVERALL

First proof variations (Far left) This reproduction has a bias of cyan and yellow, making the neutrals green. The red chair now looks brown.
(Left) This is too light overall, and the reflections on the table top have been lost completely.

TOO MAG AND CYAN

LACKS DETAIL

FILMS TRANSPOSED

Color proof correction: jewelry

First proof variations (Left) The magenta and cyan are too strong, causing the grays to go mauve and the golds bronze. (Below left) Here, the color balance is correct but the picture lacks detail. Although the numbers on the faces of the watches are distinct enough, the black is too flat to give the picture the modeling it needs. (Bottom left) The cyan and magenta films have been transposed – i.e. the cyan film has been printed with magenta ink and the magenta film printed with cyan ink. Normally, this fault makes the proof look so far out that it is easy to spot.

FIRST PROOF

With jewelry shots, it is important that the original be as sharp as possible to keep the definition when reproduced.

First proof This proof does not look very sharp (**1**); the golds look dull (**2**); as does the leather strap (**3**).

Instruction to separator
Increase contrast; reduce cyan; strengthen yellow; check register and fit.

FINAL PROOF

Final proof Increasing the contrast has corrected all three faults in the first proof: the golds are a lot brighter; the leather strap is much cleaner; and the whole picture is sharper. There is far more detail and everything is legible.

Identifying the problem
Looking at the problem proof through a glass shows that it is too flat – the white line should have only a yellow dot in it.

Color proof correction: fine art

Reproducing fine art is difficult for a color house, as it will normally see only a transparency, not the original. The transparency should always be shot and reproduced with a color bar, as here.

First proof By looking at the color bar, you can see at a glance that the cyan on this proof is down. This has made all the blues (**1**), greens (**2**) and browns (**3**) look thin.

Instruction to separator
Increase cyan.

Identifying the problem In the enlargement (above) you can see the lack of cyan in the greens. With this shade of green, the dots should nearly join up.

128

SHADOWS TOO OPEN

First proof variation (Above)
The shadows are too open, and
the darker blues too light,
causing a loss of detail and
modeling.

HIGHLIGHTS POOR

First proof variation (Above)
This picture is also flat, but in this
case the highlight dots are too
large, causing a loss of detail in
the lighter areas and over-
emphasizing the slightly darker
highlights. The effect has been to
make the hands slightly green.

You could use the color bar alone
to check the correction
achieved on this proof. The grays
are now neutral; the greens are
stronger and less yellow; and the
browns are less warm.

Color proof correction: illustration

Pictures containing text, such as this (below), can tend to look flat and illegible, as it is made up of dots of all four colors.
Identifying the problem In the enlargement (right), you can see the problem. The fine lines in the picture are less than a dot in width, and thus lose definition.

FIRST PROOF

(Top) This black and white halftone is too flat, which makes the background look gray instead of white. The flatness also accounts for the loss of detail.

FINAL PROOF

(Above) Here, the dot in the background has been made smaller, thus increasing the contrast between the highlights and the midtones (i.e. 50%). This gives the image greater detail.

FINAL PROOF

The text has become far more legible and the definition of the plants has been improved by using a black line instead of tone (below). Obviously, this should be an instruction to the color house at the outset, or you will be charged for an "author's correction."

Were the image to be enlarged, you would be able to see how the improvement has been achieved by the line shot giving enhanced detail.

FIRST PROOF

This has been reproduced using a 150 screen (right). Although this is the standard screen used for most color work, the fine line in this picture would have been helped by the use of a finer screen. Here, the edges on the leaves appear jagged and the fine lines around the bird's eye are not picking up sufficiently.

FINAL PROOF

This has been reproduced again, but this time with a 200 screen (above). The more dots there are per inch, the closer the printed result gets to continuous tone, which gives the greatest detail. The edges of the leaves now appear straight and unbroken, and the detail on the plumage is greatly enhanced.

What are the problems in reversing out and overprinting type?

TYPE SHOULD BE reversed out of as few colors as possible. Any type matter smaller than 10pt should be reversed out of one color only. This is because exact positioning cannot be guaranteed in printing.

If it is necessary to reverse out of two or more colors, it may be advisable to use the dominant color (black, for example) for the shape of the letters. However, this method can be used only when there is a solid black. If it is done with color tints, the spreading will give a halo on the colors that are not spread.

Also, whenever you use a solid black, there should be a 50% tint of cyan under it, to give a depth of color. Although it is helpful to specify this, usually the color separation house will do it anyway.

Very small letters and typefaces that are light or have serifs should not be used for reversals, as the slightest misregister (printing out of position) will result in fringes showing color in the white type areas.

The designer should also ensure that reversed-out lettering on light backgrounds is legible.

FOREIGN CO-EDITIONS In book production there are often co-editions with foreign publishers, and these can be economical only if the black plate alone is changed. Obviously if type is reversed out of one or more of the other colors this would involve changing extra plates, which could make the co-edition uneconomical.

OVERPRINTING Care should be taken by the designer when overprinting type matter that it should not merge into a light or dark background, as this will affect legibility.

Trying out type The strip of type (below) running across this spread demonstrates what works and does not work when type is reversed out of, and overprints, certain colors.

New York
New York
New York
New York
New York
New York
New York
New York
New York
New York
New York
New York
New York
New York
New York

ABCD

QRSTUVW

m nonnumy eiusmod tempor incidunt u lore magna aliqua erat volupat. Ut enin eniam, quis nostrud exercitation nisi u ra commodo consequat. Duis autem ve lor in reprehenderit in volupante velit ess nsequat, vel illum dolore eu fugiat nulla ero eos et accusam et iusto odiom dignis

Lrem ipsum dolor sit amet, consectetur adipiscing elit, sed diam zum nonnumy eiusmod tempo incidunt ut labore et dolore magna aliqua erc volupat. Ut enim ad minim veniam, quis nostrud exercitation nisi ut aliquip ex era commodo conse quat. Duis autem vel eum irure dolor in reprehenderi in volupante velit esse molestaie consequat, vel illun dolore eu fugiat nulla pariatur. At vero eos e accusam et iusto odiom dignissim qui blandi praesent luptatum delenit aigue duos dolor et se molestias excepteur sint occaecat cupidtat nor provident, simil sunt it culpa qui officia deserun mollit anim id est laborum et dolor fuga. Et harume

When is type poor?

WHEN CHECKING the quality of type on color proofs, the designer should look out for:

Type that is too weak and gray or breaking up – caused by overexposure. Type that is too strong and thickened – caused by underexposure. Paste-up marks show – caused by the paste-up not having been cleaned properly or the color separation house not "spotting" the negative to remove marks.

FINE LETTERING Thin lines, box rules, and medium and fine type matter and detail should ideally be reproduced in only one color. The use of two or more colors will make it difficult for the printer to ensure that they are exactly on top of each other, and any movement during printing (which cannot always be avoided on high-speed presses) will result in the subject being out of register, so that fringes are seen.

How do I deal with originals and proofs for packaging?

IN THIS BOOK we have dealt mainly with the litho process and with printing on paper or board. Packaging can involve other printing processes such as gravure, screen printing, or flexography, all of which are described in the introduction. It can also involve printing on glass, flexible or solid plastic, wood, metal, and other materials.

As a result of the wide range of processes and materials, there are many different ways in which artwork should be prepared and proofs checked. Because this is a specialist area, the designer needs to work much more closely with the color separation house and printer than is necessary with litho jobs.

For example, cartons that contain milk or orange juice are made out of a waterproofed board which cannot be printed by lithography and is therefore printed by flexography (see pages 28-29). In flexography, a photopolymer plate is used, and the process is such that it is difficult or impossible to show fine type. If the artwork has fine type on it, this will thicken up so as to be unrecognizable, and the same will happen to fine rules and other graphic details. Reversed-out small or fine type will tend to fill in.

PRINTING PROCESSES

Glass
Onto paper labels
- Lithographic
- Gravure
- Letterpress
- Silkscreen

Onto PVC shrink sleeves
- Gravure reverse printed
- Flexographic reverse printed

Plastic
Onto paper labels
- Processes as for glass
Shrink sleeves
- As above
Stretch labels
- As above
In mold labeling
- i.e. special type of pre-printed label inserted into bottle mold
Bottle is formed so label is fused to bottle surface

Therimage
- Heat transfer labels Gravure and screenprint Dry-offset.

Cardboard
- Lithographic
- Flexographic
- Screenprint
- Gravure

Plastic
Direct onto plastic
- Screenprint
- Flexographic

Foil/film Laminates
- Flexographic
- Gravure

Can/metal
- Dry-offset print
- Reprotherm – transfer system for full-color photographic image

Printed sheets for yogurt cartons The containers are printed on specially treated (waterproofed) board and the lids on metallic foil (left).

134

Production for packaging A few of the wide variety of techniques used in the production of packaging:

Printing self-adhesive labels for use on pharmaceutical products (top left) is done on the roll.

Checking printed labels for consistency of color (top center).

Knocking out cartons ready for gluing once they have been printed, cut, and creased (right). Here, they are being separated.

The Aesthedes system (left) enables designers to manipulate images speedily, trying out different colorways for packaging and exploring color variants. The system allows for experimentation in packaging design without having to wait for color proofs to see what the final finished product is going to look like.

A selection of plastic containers (left). The printing can either be applied directly to the surface of the plastic, using silk screen or flexography, or be offset on a self-adhesive paper label. The latter allows the use of finer detail.

A typical pack for liquids (right). This is an Elopak container made of board sandwiched between layers of polyethylene (below). Liquid packs can also be lined with foil for fruit juice packaging.

Printing on this material is either by flexography or gravure. Both these processes have limitations as regards register and the use of fine type. The designer needs to work closely with the printer to achieve good results.

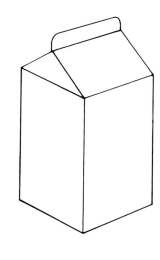

Here, the black rules around the type overlap the color area to minimize register problems and prevent white from showing around the lettering.

polyethylene

board

polyethylene

TESCO
FRESH
APPLE
FRUIT
FILLING

TESCO

FRESH
— APPLE —
FRUIT FILLING

Lightly stewed apple, delicious with cream or custard. Ideal as a pie filling. All the taste of fresh apples in a convenient pack.

500 g ℮

0256 02025**7** 020258
0259   2

PURE-PAK™

OPEN OTHER SIDE

INGREDIENTS:
Apple, Water, Sugar, Modified Starch, Glucose Syrup.

TESCO QUALITY
If you are not entirely satisfied with any Tesco product, please return it to the store where it was purchased where we will be pleased to replace it. Or send it with the packaging to the Consumer Relations Manager at the following address, stating where and when it was purchased. This offer does not affect your statutory rights.
PRODUCED IN THE U.K. FOR TESCO STORES LTD., CHESHUNT, ENB 9SL © TESCO '89 **0477**

NUTRITION

A serving = approx. ¼ of the carton		
TYPICAL COMPOSITION	A 125g (4½ oz) serving provides	100g (3½ oz) provide
Energy	314 kJ/ 75 kcal	251 kJ/ 60 kcal
Protein	0.3g	0.2g
Carbohydrate of which sugars	19.4g 16.5g	15.5g 13.2g
Fat	0g	0g
Fibre	1.6g	1.3g
VITAMINS/ MINERALS	% RECOMMENDED DAILY AMOUNT	
Vitamin C	26%	

THIS PACK CONTAINS 4 SERVINGS

INFORMATION

A color control bar to check density of ink and other printing characteristics (see page 70-71).

Type needs to be bold and clean (preferably sans serif) on this form of packaging and at least 8pt size. Some examples of typefaces that pose problems are shown right.

Register and trim marks.

These packs (right) are printed by offset on standard packaging board, and the design limitations of flexography and gravure do not apply.

Some of these packs use an uncoated board, which means that a coarser screen (120 or so) will have to be used.

AB

ABCD

A B C

Aa Bb

Aa Bb Cc

Some color house nightmares

Moiré Moiré pattern (above) is unsightly but sometimes impossible to avoid, unless the designer can find a different subject.

There are certain subjects or requests that are notoriously difficult and expensive for the color house to achieve. Most color houses will attempt to do them, but the cost will obviously reflect the amount of work involved and the sheer difficulty of achieving a good result.

Just a few are shown on this spread!

Hairline cut out Cutting out around a hairline (above) is difficult and time consuming, particularly if (as here) the hair tends to merge into the background, rather than being shot on a light background. The color house will charge much more to do this than a straightforward cut out.

Gold lamé One of the trickiest of fabrics to reproduce (above). The gold, shiny quality of lamé is difficult to convey in a way that is true to the subject. Help your color house by sending them a fabric swatch with the color transparency.

Bicycle cut out The same applies here (left), only more so. The sheer amount of work and time required to cut out between the spokes of the wheels is horrendous!

Black on black Black patterning on a black dress is very difficult to achieve, as the scanner really has nothing to pick up to give the required contrast (above). There is not a cost problem here, just the difficulty in giving the required result.

White detailing Retaining the brilliant whiteness of the dress, which is really paper white, while trying to hold the modeling of all the pleats and folds, is difficult (below).

This modeling can be created only by dots of the four colors, and there is a danger that these will "dirty" the white. At best, the color house can achieve only a compromise.

Lack of clear instructions Another nightmare for the color house is when the designer has written an essay on every single subject, rather than giving concise, clear instructions (above). The color house is left with the time-consuming task of reading all the comments and converting them into proper color corrections.

Sending material in small batches A pet hate of color houses (and probably designers) is breaking a job up into small batches. Every time a batch comes in, the color house has to pick up the job again. When the batches are all at different stages, it is difficult to keep track of where material is, and batching can often mean "more haste, less speed."

Glass mounts Opening a package of transparencies that have been left in their glass mounts, and which have broken in transit, is a color house's nightmare: the splinters of glass will almost certainly have scratched the transparencies (above).

Ten golden rules

1 Specify tints in percentages, not Pantone colors.

2 Do not try to bluff if you lack technical knowledge. Admit it and ask for help.

3 The better the original, the better the proof.

4 Realize that the process cannot yield perfection. If a proof is very nearly right, do not correct.

5 Take care with fine type and reversals.

6 If additional work or a major correction is required, ask the color separation house to quote before they do it.

7 Show the client and the color house finished artwork.

8 When correcting proofs, say what you want, rather than telling the color house how to do it.

9 Have the client sign off the final proof.

10 TALK to your color house.

How do I check blueprints and film?

NORMALLY, BLUEPRINTS will be supplied by the printer rather than the color house. This is because if the color house has supplied page proofs completely made-up (see pages 56-57), there is no need for them to supply a blueprint. The page film simply goes to the printer, who imposes it, so that the pages fall in the correct place on the sheet to run in sequence. In theory, all the printer can do wrong is put the pages in the wrong order or out of position. With page film, the printer should not be able to alter anything within the page. However, it is worth checking the blueprint for scratches and damage as well as for position.

Where scatter proofs have been supplied by the color house, the printer's blueprint needs much more careful checking, as the printer has done the page make-up, and it is the first time the designer sees the type and pictures together.

To make a blueprint the printer will normally proof only the black and the most predominant of the colors (yellow, for example), which means that material that appears only in magenta or cyan will not show up. Here, the designer should point out what is missing and leave it to the printer to check the film.

Sometimes the color house will supply a blueprint of a single page or picture, to show that a type correction, cropping, or positional change has been made and a revised color proof is not justified.

CHECKING FILM On most commercial or advertising jobs, the film can go straight from the color house to the printer, without the designer seeing it, particularly with page film.

The need to check film occurs mainly in bookwork, where the pictures have been scatter proofed and the text film made elsewhere by the typesetter. Here, the designer will check the film for completeness and damage and compare it with the rough paste-up, so that when the printer starts imposition, everything has been checked on the film.

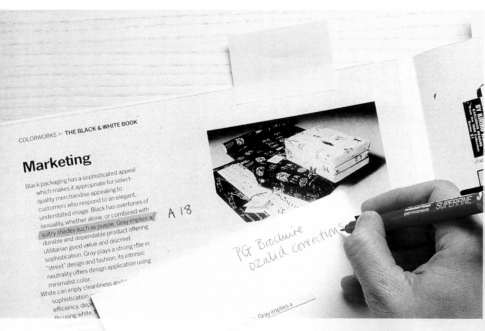

Correcting type In many cases if type is corrected at blueprint stage (to be avoided if possible), it will have to be reset and new camera-ready copy stripped in. In this instance, the typesetter should be asked to supply a "patch" of three or four lines, even if the correction affects only one line, to enable the color house to position the corrected CRC more easily. Very minor type corrections can be done by the color house. An example is the deletion of a character. However, where the deletion requires respacing between words it is better to reset.

How do I check color on press?

The vast majority of printing jobs are produced in the absence of the designer or client. However, where there is a long run of color for a book or packaging, or where the color is critical, the designer and/or client will be present, either for the first one or two sheets, or for the complete run.

This applies particularly to prestige promotional material, such as a corporate brochure or report and accounts. With such items, the designer should encourage the client to be present, and may have to insist on this. The reason is that sometimes compromises have to be made, for example with corporate colors (see pages 44-45). If the client is present, the problem and the need to compromise can be explained much more easily than after the event. If the client refuses to see such jobs on machine, it must be made clear that the designer assumes full authority to pass the job on the client's behalf without any financial penalty, should the job be criticized later.

Note that if the designer and/or client pass a job and the run is to the same standard as the sheet they have signed, the printer cannot be held responsible for any printing faults not picked up.

When making the press ready, the printer should have the marked color proofs and progressives to refer to, as well as the marked blueprint. Before passing the color, the designer should check the printed sheet against the blueprint, to ensure that any corrections have been carried out properly.

Then the sheet should be checked for spots, which can sometimes occur in the platemaking process (unless they occur in the middle of a picture, they can usually be deleted from the plate, without removing it from the machine). Register should be checked to ensure that all the color films are positioned accurately.

Finally, the color values should be checked. The color can be adjusted by regulating the amount of ink released onto the inking rollers and then onto the plate. One major problem in adjusting color on the machine is that it can be done only in "tracks" – that is, in strips parallel to the direction in which the sheets come off the machine. Therefore, if you increase the magenta in one picture, the magenta will be increased in all the other subjects in that track. Another problem occurs when the imposition dictates that the two halves of a double-page spread be in different tracks. Clearly, the two halves must match as closely as possible, without upsetting the color balance of other subjects in the two tracks.

Decisions about color adjustment need to be made quickly, either because the press is already running, or it is making ready and productive time is being lost. Checking color on machine can be an intimidating experience until the designer has done it several times. However, the printer will usually advise and help the novice on how to achieve the best result.

Index

Quarto would like to thank the following for their help with this publication and for permission to reproduce copyright material. Special thanks must go to Art Directors Photo Library for all their help; and Peter Brehm of SWOP.

KEY: a = above, b = below, c = center, r = right, l = left

Credits

Every effort has been made to trace and acknowledge all copyright holders. Quarto would like to apologise if any omissions have been made.